Young People's Perspectives on Education, Training and Employment

The Future of Education from 14+ Series

Series Editors: Ann Hodgson and Ken Spours

THE FUTURE OF EDUCATION FROM 14+

Young People's Perspectives on Education, Training and Employment

Realizing their potential

**Lorna Unwin and
Jerry Wellington**

Routledge
Taylor & Francis Group

LONDON AND NEW YORK

First published 2001 by Routledge

2 Park Square, Milton Park, Abingdon, Oxfordshire OX14 4RN
52 Vanderbilt Avenue, New York, NY 10017

Routledge is an imprint of the Taylor & Francis Group, an informa business

First issued in paperback 2020

British Library Cataloguing in Publication Data

A CIP record for this book is available from the British Library.

ISBN 978-0-7494-3122-8 (hbk)
ISBN 978-0-367-60496-7 (pbk)

Typeset by Routledge

Contents

Contents

Series editors' foreword

As full-time 16+ staying-on rates reached a peak in the mid-1990s, policy makers and researchers concerned with initial post-compulsory education and training began to turn their attention to the role of apprenticeship and the work-based route for 16–19 year olds. Over the last five years there have been several research projects focusing on the emerging modern apprenticeships, which were launched in 1995. However, the outputs from this work have tended to have been confined to official government reports and have not been published in a form that can be accessed by a wider readership. In general, the whole area of work-based training remains an under-researched and under-theorized area and still rather marginal in terms of policy debates. We therefore very much welcome this book as a major contribution to the debate about learning in the workplace. Its particular strength is that it captures the voices of the young people themselves as they make choices about their future lives and as they progress through initial post-compulsory education and training in the workplace.

This is the second book to explore issues around work-based training in this series on the future of education and training at 14+. We make no apology for revisiting this theme, both because there is a shortage of contemporary accounts of young people's experience in education and training and because of the potentially important role their perceptions can and should play in shaping the future development of the post-16 field.

The focus of this book on young people and their views about post-16 education and training provide, therefore, a refreshingly new slant on the issue of work-based learning for policy makers, researchers and practitioners. We hear about the problems of choosing the most appropriate pathway at 16+ through what is still a very complicated and confusing set of options. A significant proportion of young people actively chooses the work-based route at this stage and they are very clear that this is the right choice for them. However, from the authors' research it appears that many of them, particularly the high-achieving ones, are actively discouraged by their teachers from contemplating entering the work-based route at 16. This book thus provides convincing evidence of continuing prejudice and ignorance about what the workplace can offer as a site of learning, despite the increasing importance of skill building for the future.

What emerges from the book is a strong case for the development of a high-quality apprenticeship system and the forging of closer links between education and the world of work. However, while celebrating the potential of work-based learning, this book is very critical of many of its current realities. It argues that both policy and practice have a long way to go to satisfy the aspirations of many young people.

At present, modern apprentices often find that their learning experience in the workplace falls short of what they had expected and what the policy makers suggest they ought to be receiving. For example, young people are often left very isolated in the workplace and are unclear to whom they should turn for support. Moreover, the quality of their experiences is still very variable and there is not a common sense across the United Kingdom of what it means to be a modern apprentice. Despite the developments in modern apprenticeships carried out by both the current and the previous administrations, qualification completion rates in these programmes remain stubbornly low. The book cuts through much of the policy rhetoric and paints a picture of a partially fulfilled promise to young people.

The book is both focused and comprehensive in its scope. Apprenticeship is the central theme, but the authors range more widely and embrace other topical areas such as key skills, foundation degrees, Curriculum 2000 and the introduction of learning and skills councils. The authors begin with an up-to-date review of recent policy initiatives in the post-16 field and finish with a number of recommendations for improving the quality of the educational experience for this very important section of the 16–19 year old cohort. The book argues for a strong and respected work-based route, which will fulfil its potential as both a means of transition to working life and also as a possible route into further study.

Ann Hodgson and Ken Spours
Series editors

Preface

The aim of this book is to present young people's conceptions of and perspectives on a range of issues connected to learning and its relationship to
employment and the world of work. These include issues such as the connection of schooling to employment; the meaning of personal effectiveness;
the role of core or key skills and the issue of transfer; the academic/voca-
tional divide; the connection between workplace learning and learning in
institutional settings (such as schools, colleges and places where training is
provided); the 'situated' nature of skills and knowledge; and, more generally, the purpose of education and training and the future of work. Those
views are compared and contrasted with the statements and documents of
policy makers, politicians, curriculum planners and others that shape and
administer education, training and employment. These comparisons and
contrasts indicate that, on occasions, the varying perspectives directly conflict, at other times they may agree, and on other occasions the two sets of
views on the same area are totally disconnected – with one set sometimes
guilty of committing what Gilbert Ryle (1949) called a 'category mistake'.

The perspectives of young people are compared with the critical literature
related to the issues under discussion. Here, a similar process is applied. In
some cases the literature supports one conception or perspective rather than
another – in other cases it may be disconnected and may even appear dys-
functional. We feel that this 'triangular' way of presenting evidence and
structuring data may be a useful strategy for the application and dissemina-
tion of research, and of showing its value to a range of interested parties
including policy makers, curriculum planners, teachers/trainers and others.
In the final chapter we try to tease out some of the implications of the book
for policy and practice. There we hope to show that the voices presented,
and their contrast and connection with other perspectives, can give valuable
insights into policy and its construction, into curriculum planning and
development, and into the practice of teaching and training.

The young people presented here include boys and girls from the ages of
10 to 16, and young men and women between the ages of 16 and 22. Their
voices arise out of interview data gathered from tape-recorded individual
and small-group interviews and from young people's written answers to our
questions. Our contention is that some express their views as well in writing
as others do in speech, hence the value of relying on two methods of collecting data. Their written and spoken views have been recorded during the
course of a number of projects, jointly carried out by the two authors. Most

of the data emanate from our work as part of the national evaluation of the modern apprenticeship programme in the United Kingdom from 1994 to 1995, and from a follow-up study of apprentices, which we carried out independently from 1996 to 1999. These young people offer a unique perspective as they inhabit the small but still significant work-based pathway in the English post-16 landscape. Although the majority of young people now stay in full-time education after the age of 16, some 30 per cent take a different route either through choice, as a consequence of under-achievement or other restrictions, or because they have become disaffected with the formal system. The apprentices in our study had a choice. Most of them had achieved sufficient passes at 16 to enable them to stay in full-time education. They chose instead to combine work and study.

Other data in the book arise from an evaluation we were commissioned to do of a curriculum initiative on 'personal effectiveness' for school and college students in the north-west of England in 1996. We use this research to expand a discussion of the role and meaning of key skills.

Some details and analysis of the projects themselves have been included in this book (see Unwin and Wellington, 1995, and Unwin and Wellington, 1997 for the full project reports). Rather than providing a detailed anatomy of a particular project, however, the book aims to give printed space to the voices of young people on a range of issues that are of international importance and interest. The contrast and comparison of those voices and views with current education, training and employment policy, political rhetoric and the discourse of official documents form the central theme of the book.

We are not claiming that the voices we have presented here are typical or representative of young people as a whole. We have selected them because of their insights and relevance to current debates about learning in different contexts and to the policymaking process. The very act of selection, of course, is fraught with danger. Not only did we select young people to interview and survey for our various research projects, we have also carried out further layers of selection as we dissected our research data. Hodkinson *et al* (1996, p 157), in their book on young people's approaches to career decision-making, remind us: 'As is the case in all such research, the resulting text is a construction, arising from our own interpretations of what was said to us.' We acknowledge that our own voices, as well as actions, as researchers have the most power here. We hope, however, that by presenting what young people have said to us through the use of substantive sections of interview and survey data, the reader will be able to 'hear' the young people and that their voices have not been drowned by our own.

1

Young people and post-16 education and training policy

Introduction

Each generation of young people faces, in some ways, a different future from their predecessors. Young people today, in the developed world at least, are bombarded with prophetic claims about the end of manual labour and the rise of the knowledge economy, the need for everyone to be lifelong learners, the domination of technology, the globalization of capital, and even the end of work. Ashton and Green (1996, p 70) point out that 'The remarkable thing about these claims is that they are typically presented with relatively little theoretical grounding and even less of a basis in solid empirical evidence.' Such problems do not appear, however, to concern policymakers who chant the litany of change in a mantra-like fashion at every opportunity. Thus, in its 1999 White Paper proposing changes to the structure and funding of post-16 education and training, the UK's Labour government declared:

> The challenge we face to equip individuals, employers and the country to meet the demands of the 21st century is immense and immediate. In the information and knowledge-based economy, investment in human capital – in the intellect and creativity of people – is replacing past patterns of investment in plant, machinery and physical labour. To continue to compete, we must equip ourselves for this new world with new and better skills. We must improve levels of knowledge and understanding and develop the adaptability to respond to change.
>
> (DfEE, 1999a, p 12)

Prime Minister Tony Blair, in a foreword to a report on social exclusion, spelt out the message for young people: 'A few decades ago only a minority stayed in education until 18 or 21. But as we move into an economy based more on knowledge, there will be ever fewer unskilled jobs. For this generation, and for young people in the future, staying at school or in training until 18 is no longer a luxury. It is becoming a necessity.' (SEU, 1999, p 8).

In addition to hammering out the mantra of a changing world, both the above statements bind together the individual and the nation state in accepting a shared responsibility to meet the challenge ahead. This follows in the footsteps of policy documents since the early 1980s, which have linked together young people's so-called lack of employability skills and the nation's poor economic performance. For example, in his critique of the 1986 White Paper, *Working Together – Education and Training*, which said that young people lacked sufficient motivation and awareness of the realities of working life and so were unattractive to employers, Stronach (1989; p 12) noted that:

> ...the White Paper is typical in that it offers an intense personification of the problem, both at individual and national level. The direct mediation of the problem between individual attributes and national destinies sets up a simple logic locating responsibility in the attributes of an aggregate of individuals – a highly voluntarist and individualistic theory of development, in which groups are no more than the aggregate of individuals.

Fourteen years on, young people are still being told that they need to improve their employability skills (despite the fact that many UK teenagers are well acquainted with the world of work a long time before they leave school – see Chapter 2) in order to help UK plc become more profitable. Such exhortation is never tempered, however, with information that young people might find useful and interesting. For example, the policy documents do not inform young people about the fragility of the youth labour market, which is particularly vulnerable to the cyclical problems of economic recession and expansion, and to occupational restructuring (see Ashton, Maguire and Spillsbury, 1989, and Roberts, 1995). Nor do they speak about the stubborn inequalities in a youth labour market that is still, in many sectors, stratified along class, gender and race faultlines.

In this chapter, we explore the education, training and employment options open to young people in one part of the UK, England, and the real challenges they face as they attempt to make the transition to adulthood. This chapter is intended, therefore, to paint a picture of the landscape inhabited by the young people whose voices we hear throughout the rest of the book.

One of the problems that educational researchers face in England is knowing when to draw the line with regard to being 'up to date'. As we write this book, the education and training landscape is changing, just as it has been doing year by year for the past two decades. By the time this book is published, 14 year olds will be once again able to choose vocational as well as academic subjects to study in school. Some pupils, as young as 12, will be spending part of the week outside school in work experience or community-based projects in an attempt to prevent them from becoming 'disaffected'. The names of a range of courses and programmes will be changed in order to give them more status; for example, general national vocational qualifications (GNVQs) will become vocational A-levels and the modern apprenticeship will be split into a foundation and an advanced programme. These changes could be said to indicate a growing awareness from government that the country needs to reform its education and training provision for young people. On the other hand, it could be a further reflection of government failure to tackle deep-seated problems that any amount of re-branding of courses and special measures will do little to solve.

As Hodgson and Spours (1999) point out, the New Labour government, elected in 1997, inherited an education and training system that excluded large sections of young people and in which participation rates beyond the age of 16 had ceased to expand. Three years on, many initiatives have been introduced to tackle social exclusion, to raise standards in schools, to expand further and higher education, and to help unemployed people gain access to education and training. The emphasis throughout has been on full-time education.

The post-16 landscape

Each summer, schools, colleges, training providers and employers compete to capture the 16 and 17 year olds on offer. The origins of this annual market have been well documented (see, inter alia, Ball *et al,* 1999; Unwin, 1999; Felstead and Unwin, 1999; Huddleston and Unwin, 1997; Ainley and Bailey, 1997; Gleeson *et al,* 1996). Brown (1997, p 745) has shown how, at school level, marketization has meant a surge away from the 'ideology of meritocracy' to the 'ideology of parentocracy' in which educational selection is based on 'the wealth and wishes of parents rather than the individual abilities and efforts of pupils'. For young people, the knowledge that they will have to enter this market place probably has a serious impact from the age of 14 onwards. Between 14 and 16, young people will engage in a period of work experience (for one or two weeks) with a local employer, and will receive advice and guidance about their post-16 options from a representative of the Careers Service. They will also receive advice from their teachers, parents and friends.

Unwin (1999, p 16) has described the English post-16 landscape as 'jungle-like' and Evans *et al* (1997, p 5) bemoaned the fact that 'despite numerous attempts at reform over the past 15 years, provision for young people remains fragmented and incoherent, with a number of competing pathways of varying status and value'. The young people whose voices we hear in this book describe, in Chapter 3, how they chose to follow one of the pathways and confirm the view of Evans *et al* (1997) that school leavers find they are faced with anything but a level playing field.

Successive governments since 1991, when the White Paper, *Education and Training for the 21st Century* (DES/DOE, 1991) laid out a triple-track qualifications system based on A-levels, GNVQs and NVQs, have tried to

place young people within one of three pathways: academic; general vocational; and work based. The 1996 Dearing *Review of 16-19 Qualifications*
recommended that these pathways be maintained, albeit within one
national framework, and, furthermore, that their 'distinguishing character-
istics' be accentuated. (Dearing, 1996, p 15). Campaigners for a more uni-
fied approach to educational provision for 16–19 year olds were
disappointed with Dearing and clutched at the straw of the national framework in the hope that the report had not closed the door completely on a
merging of the pathways (see Hodgson and Spours, 1997, for a detailed critique of the unification debate). To some extent their optimism has been
rewarded as, from September 2000, structural changes to A-levels and
GNVQs mark, according to Hodgson and Spours (1999, p 111) 'a small
first step in the direction of the more flexible, coherent and inclusive 14–19
qualifications system' that New Labour had outlined in its pre-election
report, *Aiming Higher*. It should be remembered, however, that the Labour
government has confirmed its commitment to academic A-levels as the 'gold
standard'. The education minister, Baroness Blackstone, when announcing
the Curriculum 2000 changes, said, 'In encouraging greater breadth of
study, we are in no way compromising on depth. I have made clear from day
one that A level standards must be maintained – and, where necessary,
enhanced' (DfEE, 1999b). Students in post-16 full-time education should,
therefore, have more opportunity for building a broader portfolio of courses
and qualifications.

Full-time education is, however, only one of five pathways down which
young people might walk after the age of 16:

1. Continue in full-time education in school, sixth form college or further
   education college to study for academic and/or vocational qualifications.
2. Seek employment (full-time or part-time).
3. Enter a government-supported training programme.
4. Enter part-time education or part-time work, or combine the two.
5. Become a 'non-participant' in the education, training and employment
   system.

In Chapter 3, we discuss the way in which young people react to this landscape. We are particularly concerned in this book with the positioning of
pathway one (full-time education) in relation to pathways two and three
(employment; and government-supported training).

Part of the complexity of the UK's post-16 landscape comes from the fact
that each pathway splits into a number of tracks. In 1999, 70.7 per cent of
16 year olds followed the first pathway (full-time education), of whom 28.5
per cent did so in state schools, 6.2 per cent in independent schools, and
36.1 per cent in further education colleges (DfEE, 2000a). The majority of
these students (36.9 per cent) were taking academic A-levels, whereas the
rest studied for general national vocational qualifications (GNVQs) (15.8

per cent), and national vocational qualifications (NVQs) and other equivalent vocational qualifications (14.6 per cent). A tiny proportion (2.9 per cent) were studying for or re-sitting general certificate of secondary education (GCSE) courses, which are normally completed before the end of compulsory schooling. As we saw from Baroness Blackstone's comments above, A-levels still top the hierarchical structure in post-16 full-time education.

The 8.2 per cent of 16 year olds who entered government-supported training are split into three programmes: modern apprenticeship; national traineeship; and what the government currently terms 'other training', which embraces work experience and/or workshop based provision for young people who cannot find places with employers, and the remains of the youth training (YT) scheme. Just as with the academic pathways above, there is a clear hierarchy here led by the modern apprenticeship.

Even the pathway that takes young people straight from school into employment splits into two. In 1999, 3.1 per cent of 16 year olds went into jobs with training funded by their employer (as opposed to the government-supported pathway described above) and some 8 per cent went into jobs where no formal training was recorded. Many young people are, of course, working part-time before they reach school leaving age. Figures for 1999 estimate that 50 per cent of 16 year olds in full-time education were in employment. A rather obscure pathway (4.8 per cent in 1999) covers young people attending private colleges and training centres (for example, specialists in secretarial or language courses), and those attending any sort of college (independent or public sector) to study part-time, some of whom may be employed.

The final pathway covers young people who are not engaged in any form of education or formal training, and who are officially deemed to be economically inactive. This is a difficult category from both a quantitative and qualitative perspective. Pearce and Hillman (1998) remind us that estimating the true numbers in this category is highly problematic as the relevant agencies (DfEE, Careers Service, Labour Force Survey, Youth Cohort Study) collect their data in different ways. The generally accepted figure for non-participation is estimated to be around 9 per cent for 16 year olds in England (SEU, 1999). Regionally, however, the figure can be much higher, for example in parts of north-west and north-east England. In their ground-breaking study of the group that they called 'status zero' in South Wales, Instance et al (1994) found that between 16 and 23 per cent of 16 and 17 year olds could be found to be disengaged from education, training and employment. Increasing numbers of young people experience non-participation well beyond school leaving age through being permanently or temporarily excluded from school (see Smith, 1998).

The statistics are important in exposing the spatial differences behind a national snapshot but they tell us little about the nature of the 'non-participation'. Some of these young people could, of course, be economically active in the informal labour market working, for example, on building sites and with family businesses where their presence is not officially recorded. Some may be prevented from engaging in the activity of their choice or excluded in other ways through a physical or mental disability. Some may be suffering ill health, some may have been made homeless, and, given the significant number of teenage pregnancies in England, there will be young women whose participation is halted by caring for children. There will also be some young people who have purposefully chosen to disengage from the system.

The route to non-participation lies in social class, ethnic background, gender, educational attainment, and geographical location. Drawing on data from the Youth Cohort Study, Pearce and Hillman (1998) argue that the best predictor of participation in education and/or employment is attainment of high grades at GCSE. Children from the higher socio-economic groups are more likely to be in full-time education than those with parents in manual jobs and young people with learning difficulties and/or physical disabilities are over-represented in the non-participation group. Ethnicity has an impact in that there is high unemployment among Afro-Caribbean youths, although black and Asian young people are more likely than their white peers to stay in full-time education. The impact of gender is complex. More young women stay in full-time education at 16 (74.5 per cent in 1999, compared to 67.2 per cent of males), but slightly more of them make up the non-participation group where over half of the women are engaged as parents or caring for a relative (SEU, 1999). Deprived areas of the country account for much higher levels of non-participation. In some parts of England, more than 50 per cent of 16 year olds achieve five or more higher grade GCSE passes, whereas in others less than 30 per cent do so.

In 1999, the government's Social Exclusion Unit published a report to address non-participation and in which it acknowledged that '16 is a critical point when, for some, problems that have been brewing for years reach a crisis, and for others, problems begin that could have been avoided' (SEU, 1999, p 8). The report's solutions were to:

- introduce the concept of 'graduation' on the lines of the American high school tradition;
- improve the coherence of post-16 provision by offering three pathways – full-time general education in school or college, vocational education (in college or the workplace) and part-time education for those in jobs without training;
- introduce financial support to encourage young people from low-income families to stay in full-time education after 16;
- establish a new advice and guidance support service (Connexions) which brings together all the agencies that work with young people.

We will return to these strategies in the concluding chapter and examine the extent to which they would bring about the changes demanded by the young people we interviewed for our research.

A further important factor that needs to be remembered when considering the post-16 landscape is that the figures given above change for 17 and 18 year olds. In 1999, participation in full-time education dropped from 70.7 per cent at 16 to 58.1 per cent at 17, and to 36.8 per cent at 18. As a consequence, participation in government-supported training and employment rose, but so too did the number of young people not engaged in formal education and training (to 20 per cent at age 17, and 39.8 per cent at age 18). The volatility of the pathways is partly fuelled by poor attainment as young people fail to achieve the necessary level to progress to the second year of a course or programme. It is also fuelled by changing interests, disappointments with the chosen pathway, and, more generally, disruptions in young people's lives. Up to a third of 16–18 year olds in full-time education fail to complete their course, less than half progress from intermediate to advanced level, and only a third of trainees on government-supported training programmes leave with a complete qualification.

It is clear that many young people are struggling to find an appropriate pathway and that the pathways themselves require attention.

Re-engineering the landscape

Unlike their peers in continental Europe, young people in the UK have only recently embraced staying in school until the age of 18. Until 1987, the majority of young people left school at the earliest opportunity. In the post-war period up until the late 1970s, jobs were easy to find and employers happily recruited school leavers. Bynner's (1998) analysis of the National Child Development Study has shown, for example, that two-thirds of the cohort members born in 1958 left school at 16 and entered the labour market with relative ease. The pattern began to change with the economic downturn of the late 1970s and early 1980s, which led to a steep rise in youth unemployment, the collapse of traditional apprenticeships, and the introduction of a series of government-supported training schemes, hastily designed in response to the crisis. By 1981, the national youth unemployment rate for those under 25 was 21.4 per cent compared with 2.4 per cent in 1960 (see Ashton, 1986). In 1983 a one-year programme, the Youth Training Scheme (YTS), was introduced as an attempt to consolidate government policy on youth unemployment by putting the emphasis on 'training' as opposed to simply providing something for unemployed young people to do whilst they waited to find work.

In 1986, YTS was extended to two years and its outcomes strengthened to include the achievement of a nationally recognised vocational qualification. The state paid the trainees a weekly 'training allowance', although this was often below the normal rate being paid for the jobs that the trainees were doing. It should be noted that some employers enhanced the training allowance to bring it in line with their established wage scales. In 1988, 16 and 17 year olds lost their right to claim social security benefits ('the dole') and, instead, were 'guaranteed' a YTS place. When the Training and Enterprise Councils (TECs) were established from 1990 onwards, replacing the Employment Department's local area offices, they inherited the YTS 'guarantee'. Some TECs, notably in the north-east of England, on Merseyside, and in some rural areas, faced considerable problems trying to find placements with employers and many trainees find themselves in a period of limbo, registered with a training provider. Coles (1995, p 38), drawing on the work of Raffe (1986) describes how YTS soon settled into a stratified scheme with 'the most prestigious and sought-after schemes... run by employers' at one end of a spectrum which had, at the other end, a 'detached' sector, 'often run by local authorities or charities and based in workshops or training centres'.

The variable quality of YTS provision soon attracted criticism. Apart from the fact that some young people spent some or all of the scheme with a training provider rather than an employer, the employer-led sector was itself unreliable. In order to encourage employers to support the scheme, successive governments adopted a 'flexible' approach to regulation. This allowed employers a good deal of freedom to run their own variants of YTS. Hence, as Roberts (1995) has argued, some employers used the scheme as a lengthy selection opportunity, taking on more trainees than they needed in order to select the best, whilst some created temporary low-grade jobs in order to benefit from this pool of free labour. The 'revolving door' scenario in which young people moved from one scheme to another without ever finding a permanent job further damaged the image of YTS. The voluntarist approach underpinning YTS is at odds with the highly regulated models of youth training in most other European countries, and this continues to the present day. Its consequences permeate much of this book as we hear young people discuss the variability of their experience on the modern apprenticeship.

At the end of their review of New Labour's education and training agenda for young people and adults, published some two years after the New Labour government was elected, Hodgson and Spours (1999, p 146) concluded that: 'New Labour's current concept of the Third Way in post-14 education and training, marked by a pervasive voluntarism, does not provide an adequate agenda for future change.'

Hodgson and Spours provide an example of the way in which 'pervasive voluntarism' pollutes proactive policies. Soon after coming to power, New Labour took up a proposal advocated by Evans *et al* (1997) in their influential report *Working to Learn,* which advocated a statutory right to education and training for all young people in employment. In September 1999, the *Time for Study or Training* legislation came in, giving 16–18 year olds in employment, who had not achieved a level 2 qualification, the right to improve their education and training through either on-the-job or off-the-job provision. The legislation covered both vocational and general education qualifications and courses including: GCSE or GCE A/AS level; access courses for higher education; basic literacy and numeracy courses; and courses in 'independent living' and communication for those with learning difficulties. Yet, as Hodgson and Spours (1999, p 74) point out, the legislation did not put the onus on employers to provide training, but instead it is up to young people to seek out this entitlement. Amazingly, young people who fail to get their employer to respond to their request for time to study are expected to take the employer to a tribunal.

The decision to put all the responsibility for accessing *Time for Study* on the young person has its roots in 1970s thinking, referred to earlier, which linked economic failure to poor motivation. Such thinking reached its apotheosis in 1990, when the then Conservative government introduced the training credits initiative. The idea had originated with the Confederation of British Industry (CBI) who, in 1989, called for all young people, in full-time education and employment, to be given a 'credit' to pay for any course leading to a level 3 qualification (see CBI, 1989). At the time, the CBI saw the 'credit' benefiting two related factors: firstly an increase in jobs caused by the economic upturn of the late 1980s and, secondly, a demographic change that meant less 16 and 17 year olds would be available. The CBI (1989) claimed that the 'credit' would achieve the following benefits:

- it would provide young people with an entitlement and greater control over their development;
- increase participation as treating all young people equally would raise the status of training;
- create a market for training by turning young people into customers with buying power for whom providers would have to compete;
- offer an incentive to employers as the credit would purchase training relevant to their business needs;
- act as a powerful influence on those employers who did not normally invest in training.

The government decided to adopt the model but only for young people choosing to leave school to look for employment. In effect, this meant training credits were simply a different conduit for the funding for Youth Training (which replaced YTS in 1990). The newly established TECs (and the equivalent LECs in Scotland) were charged with introducing training credits in their areas and were given considerable freedom to package the 'credit' at local level. The story of training credits has been told in detail elsewhere (see Unwin, 1993, and Hodkinson *et al*, 1996) but it is worth dwelling briefly here on the central flaw in the whole initiative.

At the heart of the training credits concept was a bewilderingly simplistic belief that arming young people with a plastic card or voucher would enable them to persuade an employer to give them a job with training, and improve the quality of training provision in general by making providers realize they now had to compete for these newly empowered customers. Two comments from young people in Cheshire interviewed as part of Unwin's (1993) research into training credits capture the reality of the initiative as far as young people were concerned:

> I've been given this (local name for credit) card to buy a course at college but first I've got to find an employer who will let me use the card. There aren't many jobs round here so I'll be lucky to find anything decent. What happens when I get to the interview and the employer says I've got the job but doesn't mention anything about going to college? The woman from the TEC said we were supposed to tell the employer that we had the right to go to college and this card would pay for the cost. What if he says he's not interested in any card and I can take the job or leave it?
>
> (Unwin, 1993, p 206)

> I keep my card in my pocket in case anyone wants to see it and in case I can use it but so far it's stayed in its plastic wallet. I still think it's a good idea but I'm not sure the college knows what to do with it.
>
> (Unwin, 1993, p 215)

Not surprisingly, young people found that the 'credit' neither opened the doors to jobs with training nor did it make training providers any more or less responsive to their demands. The fact that between the conceptual stage at the CBI and the early 1990s when training credits became fully operational, the UK had entered another economic recession did not provide the ideal background for the initiative. Unwin (1993) found some evidence that training credits had made some young people and their parents more aware of the fact that the state provided funding to employers for the training of school leavers. Employers could still, however, opt in or out of the scheme at will.

Voluntarism has also allowed the modern apprenticeship, the supposed flagship of the UK's youth training system, to become vulnerable to the same sub-standard practices as its predecessors. It is to the modern apprenticeship that we now turn.

The modern apprenticeship

From 1988 onwards, government-supported youth training schemes found themselves in what Roberts (1995) has called the 'triple squeeze': there was a downward demographic trend; participation in full-time education beyond 16 was rising and economic recession cut the numbers of jobs for young people. By 1993, the numbers entering YT had dropped to under 300,000 from a high of 600,000 in the mid-1980s. Between 1988 and 1993, the percentage of young people staying in full-time education at 16 rose from 51.5 per cent to 70 per cent, moving from what Spours (1995) has termed a 'low participation system' to a 'medium participation system' in comparison with other European countries. Two factors appeared to have influenced the rise in participation: firstly, the reduction in the number of jobs available to school leavers and, secondly, the success of the GCSE, which had raised attainment levels and therefore encouraged young people to carry on studying (see Gray *et al*, 1993). It seemed that 16 year olds would increasingly decide to remain in full-time education and so youth training and employment figures would continue to drop. A different picture emerged, however, from 1993 onwards as the staying-on rates plateaued, even dropping back at one point to under 70 per cent, causing Hodgson and Spours (1999, p 13) to note that any growth in the initial phase of the post-compulsory education system was 'showing distinct signs of running out of steam'. It should be remembered, too, that many of the 16 year olds who did stay on only did so for one year so that participation rates were not sustained for 17 and 18 year olds.

Given that one third of young people nationally were not attracted to full-time education, providing a work-based alternative for young people remained a challenge. In addition, successive governments were still wrestling with the problem of how to increase the stock of technician level employees, which were deemed necessary to help the country compete as a trading nation. If the full-time education route was not going to produce enough people with level 3 qualifications, then the work-based route would have to play its part.

Originally announced in the 1993 November Budget Speech, the modern apprenticeship, for 16–25 year olds, was launched in September 1994 in 14 occupational sectors. Two years later, National Traineeships were launched in an attempt to improve the status of YT and to act as a progression route into apprenticeship for those young people who were not ready to enter a level 3 programme. The modern apprenticeship is now available in 82 sectors that span traditional manufacturing sectors such as engineering, steel, chemicals and glass, to services sectors such as hotel and catering, hairdressing, and retailing. (For a full list see the appendix towards the end of this volume.)

The use of the term 'apprenticeship' appeared to be a deliberate attempt to separate the new programme from the earlier schemes. Despite the fact that employer-based apprenticeships had largely disappeared in the UK due to the collapse of manufacturing industry, apprenticeship, as a concept, had retained a generally positive image in the public mind. It was equated with good-quality work-based training, with recognized vocational qualifications, with employer commitment, and was seen to offer a solid, substantive grounding in skilled occupations; everything, in fact, that youth training schemes since the late 1970s had failed to achieve (see Unwin, 1996).

Not all apprenticeships had, of course, lived up to the golden image which seemed to have lodged itself so firmly in the public consciousness (Unwin, 1996), but, nevertheless, the Conservative government of the mid-1990s was correct in assuming that the concept would still be attractive. In adding the term 'modern', the government signalled that the new programme would have some differences from the traditional model of apprenticeship. In a speech to a Confederation of British Industry (CBI) conference in December 1993, Ann Widdecombe, then Parliamentary Under Secretary of State for Employment, said: 'We do not want to stay locked into the traditional apprenticeship industries. The new model can be used anywhere and we need a real effort to involve sectors which haven't traditionally offered apprenticeship – just as we want to see them available equally to young women and men' (Widdecombe, 1993).

Given that traditional apprenticeships had largely been the preserve of white males and, in the post-Second World War era, had been mainly available in heavy manufacturing industries and construction, Widdecombe's speech appears very ambitious; some would say naive. Of course, Widdecombe and her government were launching their 'modern' apprenticeship into a very different labour market and economic context. The Conservative government's emasculation of the trades unions during the 1980s, the abolition of most of the Industrial Training Boards (ITBs), and a series of deregulation measures in industry and commerce, allowed government to design a new, 'employer friendly' model of apprenticeship, more suited to the increasingly flexible labour market. Thus the old model's requirement that apprentices should 'serve their time', which the trade unions saw as a key way to make employers honour their commitment and ensure young people completed their training, was now regarded as an anachronism.

The new model did, however, have to show that it was qualitatively different from previous and existing youth training schemes. The modern apprenticeship is based on training frameworks developed by the sector-specific national training organizations (NTOs) and leads to, as a minimum, an NVQ level 3 qualification. Some frameworks, notably in engineering and the chemical industry, also require apprentices to study for traditional (or non-NVQ) vocational qualifications, which are judged to provide the theoretical grounding missing from the NVQ. Most modern apprenticeships require young people to attend college or a training provider's premises one day per week, and in some (again, notably engineering and chemicals), apprentices spend the whole of the first year of the programme studying off-the-job. Although key skills are not a mandatory part of modern apprenticeship, they are seen by government as one way of building 'breadth' into the apprenticeship frameworks. Hence, most frameworks require apprentices to complete key skill units in communication, application of number and information technology (see Chapter 4 for a detailed discussion of key skills).

The modern apprenticeship differs from YTS and YT in other ways. Apprentices are expected to be employed (rather than be on placement from a training provider) by an employer who pays them a wage (rather than the government training allowance). Having employed status is very important to young people, as we will hear in Chapter 3.

By spring 2000, some 325,000 young people aged between 16 and 25 had joined the programme since it began in 1994. Of these, 133,000 were actually in training in 2000. Of the 82 sectors, the 15 with the most apprentices are shown in Table 1.1.

Table 1.1   Sectors with the most apprentices

Sector	Enrolled since 1995
Business administration	43,290
Engineering manufacture	31,810
Retailing	29,450
Hotel and catering	24,330
Hairdressing	24,030
Motor industry	23,110
Construction	21,860
Health and social care	18,110
Electrical installation engineering	13,060
Childcare	10,650
Accountancy	8,810
Customer services	8,370
Travel service	7,490
Information technology	6,900
Plumbing	3,700

(Source: DfEE Trainee Database System, Sheffield: Department for Education and Employment)

Drop-out rates and delayed completion are, however, causing concern. Figures for the 15 most populated sectors listed in Table 1.1 show that the percentage of young people who left the apprenticeship in 1999–2000 having completed an NVQ level 3 or above was as given in Table 1.2.

Table 1.2 Percentage of young people who left the apprenticeship in 1999–2000 having completed an NVQ level 3 or above

Sector	Percentage gaining NVQ level 3
Business administration	41
Engineering manufacture	52
Retailing	16
Hotel and catering	16
Hairdressing	29
Motor industry	49
Construction	56
Health and social care	29
Electrical installation engineering	26
Childcare	48
Accountancy	51
Customer services	26
Travel service	56
Information technology	35
Plumbing	43

(Source: DfEE Trainee Database System, Sheffield: Department for Education and Employment)

The DfEE argue that achievement of level 3 qualifications on the modern apprenticeship is improving, and that between 1998 and 1999 it increased by 11 per cent to 43 per cent. They also argue that, because apprenticeship aims at level 3 rather than the level 2 of previous youth training schemes, it is having a significant impact on the technician skills that the country has struggled to improve. Twice as many young people now leave the work-based route having achieved level 3 than did five years ago (see DfEE, 2000b). The new programme did have a mountain to climb and the achievements of many young people across all sectors should be acknowledged. The figures for retailing, customer services, hotel and catering, health and social care and electrical engineering reveal, however, that some sectors are failing to get even a third of their apprentices to level 3 before they leave the programme. The relatively low levels of achievement in the IT sector (35 per cent) are of particular concern given this sector's centrality to the modern economy.

Part of the problem could lie in having too broad a range of sectors as many do not have a tradition of substantive initial training for young people, let alone a tradition of apprenticeship (see Fuller and Unwin, 1998, and Fuller and Unwin, 1999). Some sectors are made up of small businesses that may not be able to provide the stability required to see a young person through a full apprenticeship. There are problems, too, with the requirement that apprentices complete key skills units, an issue that we discuss in detail in Chapter 4. The Training Standards Council's (TSC) chief inspector, David Sherlock, told a conference in September 1999 that his inspectors had found: lack of employer commitment to key skills; little integration of key skills, that were often taught as a block at the end of a programme; and that key skills were often the cause of dissatisfaction and non-completion (Sherlock, 1999, p 22). In addition, the modern apprenticeship has inherited some of the problems experienced by other youth training programmes, such as inadequate workplace support for trainees, poorly managed workplaces, lack of integration between on and off-the-job training and a failure to break down gender stereotyping in the workplace. The TSC report noted that, across the work-based route, 'trainee support services, as a whole, were poorly co-ordinated, so that the focus on helping trainees stay on and succeed was unclear' (Sherlock, 1999, p 10).

A further factor to be taken into consideration when examining achievement levels is that some apprentices appear to be leaving the programme prematurely but are remaining with their employer. This behaviour has historical roots in that significant numbers of apprentices in the post-war heyday of apprenticeship often completed their on-the-job training but failed to sit the exams that would have given them a vocational qualification (see Venables, 1974). Some employers clearly have little regard for qualifications. The apprentices may be glad to have a job, and may even be deploying level 3 skills, but they may come to regret not having persevered with the qualification when they need to change employer or seek a higher grade.

Despite Ann Widdecombe's aspiration that modern apprenticeships would be 'available equally to young women and men', the occupational sectors still reflect traditional divisions, an issue that we explore in more detail in Chapter 3. Thus large numbers of young men enter engineering, construction and plumbing, whereas large numbers of young women enter childcare, hairdressing and business administration. There are, however, some surprises. Some 20 per cent of apprentices in the chemical sector and 17 per cent in steel are female, but some 12 per cent of apprentices in health care and 14 per cent in the travel sector are male (DfEE, 1999b). Some sectors are approaching the stage of recruiting equal numbers of men and women: retailing; accountancy; arts and entertainment; clothing; estate agency; hotel and catering; sports and recreation; banking; customer services; and food and drink. The sectors with the most apprentices from ethnic minorities are housing (25 per cent), arts and entertainment (21 per cent), electronic systems servicing (17 per cent), guidance (14 per cent), childcare (9 per cent), retailing (7 per cent), customer service (7 per cent), information technology (7 per cent), and business administration (6 per cent). The sectors with very low ethnic minority representation are construction (1 per cent), and engineering manufacture, electrical engineering, travel service, plumbing and printing, which all stand at 2 per cent.

Despite these problems, the modern apprenticeship has the potential to revitalize the work-based route in the UK and refocus attention on important questions about the nature of formation training at technician level. The young people represented in this book saw this route as a viable alternative to staying in full-time education, and one that offered opportunities for further study as well as work experience. It remains to be seen whether the modern apprenticeship can embed itself as a respected and effective programme to which employers, young people, and society at large will give their support. The Labour government has moved to improve the programme. In February, 2000, the Secretary of State for Education and Employment announced a number of reforms that build on recommendations made by the National Skills Task Force (see NSTF, 1999):

- a clear apprenticeship structure, in which national traineeships become foundation modern apprenticeships (FMAs), leading up to advanced modern apprenticeships (AMAs);
- major improvements to the knowledge and understanding required from apprenticeship programmes, achieved by pulling together the range of technical qualifications to give clear accreditation to the underpinning skills and knowledge needed for the workplace;
- inclusion of a specified period of off-the-job learning in college, or with other training providers, with a suggested minimum of one day a week or equivalent;
- the specification of minimum periods of learning – for example two years for level 3 Modern Advanced Apprenticeships, with entry requirements tightened up (DfEE, 2000c).

He also announced a consultation process to explore 'how we can provide a coherent ladder of learning for vocational education' (DfEE, 2000c) through the following suggested options:

- guaranteed apprenticeship opportunities for 16 to 18 year olds;
- independent monitoring and support;
- financial incentives for employers and awards for trainees; and
- licensing of employers who want to engage Modern Advanced Apprentices.

Thus we see yet another change in the UK's continually evolving education and training system. We will return to Mr Blunkett's proposed improvements to the modern apprenticeship in the concluding chapter to see to what extent they will satisfy the needs and demands of young people.

The landscape's architecture

The proposed improvements to the work-based route will be taken forward by a new set of agencies that come into force in 2001. Just as the various post-16 programmes, schemes and qualifications have been subject to considerable change during the past 20 years, so too have the agencies responsible for managing and delivering them. Vast sums will no doubt be spent on new letterheads, door plates, publicity and the other trappings that are so important in establishing a 'corporate' identity.

These agencies currently include: the Careers Service, training and enterprise councils (TECs), colleges of further education, sixth-form colleges, schools, and public and private sector training providers. They meet under various so-called partnerships such as education–business partnerships, local strategic forums, and groups formed to deal with specific cross-sector initiatives such as the New Deal or New Start. For the most part, however, these organizations do not work in partnership but seek to advance their different interests (see Ball *et al*, 1999; Felstead and Unwin, 1999) and meet the targets set by their different funding bodies. Following a post-election period of consolidation when the New Labour government expressed a commitment to carrying on with most of the previous administration's policies, it is doing some landscaping of its own. In the 1999 White Paper, *Learning to Succeed*, the government explained the reasons why:

> There is too much duplication, confusion and bureaucracy in the current system. Too little money actually reaches learners and employers, too much is tied up in bureaucracy. There is an absence of effective co-ordination or strategic planning. The system has insufficient focus on skill and employer needs at national, regional and local levels. The system lacks innovation and flexibility, and there needs to be more collaboration and co-operation to ensure higher standards and the right range of choices...the current system falls short. It is incapable of delivering the improvements needed to achieve our goals.
>
> (DfEE, 1999a, p 21)

This is a damning indictment and would lead a visitor to the country to wonder why things have been allowed to get into such a mess. Part of the problem lies in the nature of the British, and, more specifically, the English policy process which, when it comes to determining the nature of the education and training system, is riddled with conflict (Richardson, 1993).

From April 2001, the post-16 landscape will change (in England) in the following ways:

IN	OUT/AMALGAMATED/NEW ROLE
Learning and Skills Council (LSC)	Further Education Funding Council (FEFC) abolished

17

Local Learning and Skills Councils (LSCs)	Training and Enterprise Councils (TECs) abolished
Local Learning Partnerships	Shift in emphasis to work under local LSCs
Connexions Strategy	Careers Services, Youth Service, voluntary organizations that currently have a responsibility for or work with young people are to come together at local level to provide an integrated service.

It is too early to say whether these new arrangements will be more effective than the existing ones. A pessimistic view is that rearranging the lifeboats on a ship that has serious engine failure may be mistaken. Amidst the chaos of civil servants and agency staff changing jobs, of new buildings being opened, and time spent ironing out bureaucratic glitches, there are thousands of young people who need the system to work better for them.

2

Listening to and talking with young people

Introduction

There is a substantial and impressive literature in this field that seeks to define and interpret the meaning of being a young person in late 20th-century society (see, inter alia, Banks *et al*, 1992; Jones and Wallace, 1992; Griffin, 1993; Coles, 1995; Coleman and Warren-Anderson, 1992; Furlong, 1992; Bates and Riseborough, 1993; Roberts, 1995; Hodkinson *et al*, 1996; Pearce and Hillman, 1998). Further work will come out of the ESRC's Youth and Citizenship Programme, which began in 1998, and the national cohort studies remain a major source of valuable data on youth transitions and family life (see Bynner *et al*, 1997; Payne, 1998). Bloomer and Hodkinson (1997) and Bloomer (1997) have added a much-needed dimension to the study of youth by exploring how young people in further education and sixth-form colleges engage with and in learning, using the concept of the 'learning career'. Ainley and Bailey (1997) also present a picture of learning in further education by contrasting students' accounts with those of college managers. And Ball, Macrae and Maguire (1999), through their research on young people in education, work and family settings in south-west London, are providing important insights into how 16–18 year olds are 'positioned very differently in terms of their opportunities and interest in the post-16 education and training market' (p 32).

In this book, we want to focus attention on what young people have to say about their experiences in education, training and employment, in order to hold those worlds up to scrutiny, rather than the young people themselves. This is not a book on *youth* as such. In a sense, we want to turn conventional youth research on its head. By listening to and talking with young people about a range of issues, we want to present their views as a contribution to a number of ongoing and crucially important debates.

The research data used in this book have been drawn from three projects, which we carried out between 1994 and 1999 in England. In each project, we sought the views of young people on a range of issues related to education, training, workplace learning and employment. We personally conducted all of the fieldwork for the projects and, in many cases, visited sites together in order to jointly interview young people. The projects were as follows:

1. Evaluation of young people's experiences as apprentices in the pilot year of Modern Apprenticeship (1994–1995), funded by the Department for Education and Employment (DfEE) (see Unwin and Wellington, 1995).
2. Follow-up study of a sample of apprentices from 1995–9, funded by the Centre for Research in Post-Compulsory Education and Training at the University of Sheffield.
3. Evaluation of young people's experiences of participating in a curriculum initiative to develop 'personal effectiveness' skills in schools and colleges, funded by the South and East Cheshire Education Business Partnership in 1995/1996 (see Unwin and Wellington, 1997).

Projects 1 and 3 are similar: both were evaluative in nature, and were generated and externally funded by clients wanting to know if their pilot initiatives were working; both required the evaluators to gather quantitative and qualitative data; and both were carried out within a specified timescale. In the case of the follow-up study of apprentices (project B), we had complete freedom to design and implement the research and to use the data for our own purposes. It should be noted, however, that, despite being externally funded evaluators, we had considerable freedom within projects 1 and 3 with regard to research methods and sampling, and in being able to publish our findings separately from the final reports produced for the clients. We discuss the nature of our roles as evaluators and the evaluation process in more detail below.

Any attempt to describe and categorize the young people presented in this book is problematic. We can, however, present a picture of sorts for the reader by dividing the young people into two groups as follows:

Group one: the apprentices

The apprentices involved in projects 1 and 2 were located in the following areas of England: Yorkshire; Lincolnshire; Hertfordshire; Devon; Merseyside; Cheshire; and Greater Manchester. For project 1, we surveyed, by questionnaire, 350 apprentices during the first year of their apprenticeship, and carried out interviews with 120. For project 2, we carried out a series of follow-up interviews with 80 of the original 120 apprentices.

The apprentices ranged in age from 16 to 21 and had all attended state schools. They included slightly more males than females and the vast majority were white, with some 2 per cent from ethnic minorities. Some 3 per cent of the apprentices declared themselves to have a disability. The apprentices were employed in the following occupational sectors: engineering manufacture; steel; retailing; childcare; information technology; chemicals; and business administration.

The majority of apprentices had GCSE attainment levels that were well above the national average in that 60.6 per cent had achieved five or more GCSE passes at grade C and above. Within that group, there was a substantial sub-set (35 per cent) with five or more GCSE passes at either grade A or B. The sector with the highest number of apprentices achieving five or more GCSEs at grade C and above is steel (86.7 per cent), followed closely by polymers (84.6 per cent), chemicals (80.5 per cent) and travel services (77.8 per cent). The least qualified apprentices were in engineering construction and electrical installation engineering. Using GCSE measures, male apprentices were generally better qualified than females.

A significant number (12.4 per cent) of apprentices had completed A-level courses. The most commonly taken subjects were mathematics, physics and chemistry. The highest percentage of apprentices who completed A-levels were to be found in information technology and polymers. A small number of apprentices (6.3 per cent) had completed a GNVQ course. Some (18.1 per cent) had also achieved a vocational qualification prior to becoming apprentices. The majority of apprentices had had a gap (varying from one month to five-and-a-half years) between leaving full-time education and entering the apprenticeship.

Their parents reflected all types of employment background from so-called unskilled through to professional. Some parents were unemployed and some owned their own businesses. The vast majority of apprentices lived in the family home.

The apprentices' earnings varied considerably, with the lowest on a weekly wage of £35 and the highest on £165. The two highest paid occupational sectors were engineering and agriculture. The lowest paid sector was childcare. Male apprentices, on average, earned more money than females. The better qualified (in GCSE terms) the apprentice, the higher the weekly wage.

Group two: the full-time students

Young people in this group were located in state primary (age 10–11) and secondary schools (age 11–16), and in one college of further education (age 16–18) in urban and rural Cheshire. They included slightly more females than males, and some 3 per cent were from ethnic minority backgrounds. As with the apprentices, family backgrounds varied enormously. The college students were studying for A-levels in a range of subjects, and for GNVQs in business administration and art and design. The secondary school students were studying at various stages of the national curriculum and one group was in the first year of their GCSE programme.

We acknowledge that these composite sketches ignore hugely complex variations in the young people's life experiences: some of them will have spoken from a background of financial privilege; others from an unhappy family background from which the workplace, school or college has provided an escape, whereas some may have gained a foot on a ladder that will take them well away from the stereotyped futures other people had mapped out for them. In their seminal study, *Youth and Inequality*, Bates and Riseborough (1993, p 2) remind us that 'In the UK, social class remains the major determinant of relative social mobility...and the labour market and labour process remain deeply gendered and racist.' Yet, they also argue that 'At all levels, many young people showed a notable degree of reflexivity, a capacity for creative reconstruction of biography in terms of personal progress and fulfilment' (Bates and Riseborough, 1993, p 6). We would argue that by tapping into this capacity for reflexivity, we have garnered a store of valuable insights from young people that could be used to critically question a range of policies related to education, training and employment.

The nature of 'pilot' schemes and the evaluation of pilots

As we noted above, much of the research data included in this book was drawn from two evaluation studies that external agencies contracted us to carry out. There has been a considerable growth in evaluation studies funded by government departments and quasi-governmental organizations in the 1980s and 1990s. This has been particularly evident in the fields of education and training where, in the words of Stronach and Morris (1994, p 6), 'multiple innovation became the norm, with the next set of reforming initiatives overtaking and overlapping the last lot before their effect was known or knowable'. Despite the potential constraints involved in funded evaluations, many academics in university education departments have entered this world. Their reasons may include some or all of the following: they are under pressure to bring in external monies and so need to look beyond traditional sources of research; they regard funded evaluation as a means of gaining access to sites and people more easily; because funded evaluation offers opportunities to work more closely with policymakers; because they hope to play a part in improving policy design and implementation; because the evaluation will allow them to investigate certain localized initiatives for which other research funds may not be available. For a detailed discussion of the different approaches to and development of educational evaluation, see Stronach and Torrance (1995).

In our case, we decided to bid for the evaluation of modern apprenticeship because we had both been researching in the areas of youth training, school-to-work transition, and employers' attitudes and practices in relation to vocational education and training, for a number of years. We saw an opportunity in the evaluation to immerse ourselves quickly in a major new national initiative and to gain easier access to a wide range of employers, training providers and young people. The opportunity to evaluate the curriculum initiative (project 3 above) emerged part way through our apprenticeship research. At the time, this initiative, in complete contrast to the modern apprenticeship, was confined to an area in the north-west of England, was not government led, and had resulted as part of a local education–business partnership's strategy to introduce full-time students to a range of 'employability' or 'personal effectiveness' skills. Given that part of our evaluation of modern apprenticeship was to gain young people's views on key skills, achievement of which is a mandatory part of their programme, we felt that the Cheshire project might give us further insights into how such variously named 'skills' were being received and understood by young people. Data from this project are presented in Chapter 4.

Bidding for evaluation contracts means competing against the ever-increasing number of private consultancies that, in the main, can react more easily to the often ludicrously tight deadlines imposed by the 'customer'. More importantly, academic researchers can find that where they would naturally problematize the issues to be explored in an evaluation, the consultants will play a more 'conformative' role – one that sticks much more closely to the prescribed brief. How far academic researchers are forced to, or choose to, 'conform' will depend to some extent on the nature of the project, the importance they attach to it, the level of freedom they have with regard to methodology and access to research sites, and the potential for generating publishable findings. We were possibly fortunate in that, as evaluators, we had considerable freedom to work in the way we wanted. Moreover, we would argue that ways can be found to ensure both the evaluator and the customer gain from the process. In this, we agree with Stronach and Maclure (1997, pp 99–100) who argue:

> We wish to suggest that the conventional story of current evaluative research in education – fewer resources, more competition, more compromises of all sorts – is also capable of an optimistic methodological reading, and that in the constrained research conditions of postmodernity, it may be possible to envisage new concepts and practices of research that do not simply surrender to 'conformative evaluation' (Stronach and Morris, 1994) or to the general demands of 'performativity' (Lyotard, 1984).

At the end of the day, however, every evaluator has to accept that all their hard work and interesting findings may be ignored, particularly in the case of evaluating so-called pilot initiatives. The *Concise Oxford Dictionary* (1990, p 903) defines the term 'pilot' as 'an experimental undertaking or test, especially in advance of a larger one'. During the 1990s, however, education and training initiatives launched as 'pilots' have often moved seamlessly from pilot stage to acceptability before the ink was dry on the first evaluation reports. One of us has previously written about how the training credits initiative, introduced in 1990, became known as the 'pilot doomed to succeed' as it moved from small-scale to national coverage with hardly a passing glance at the data emanating from the not inconsiderable evaluation programme (see Unwin, 1993).

When young people are engaged in 'pilot' schemes, the spotlight is on them. They can become the focus of interest for local and national media, and for more than one evaluator. In the case of the modern apprenticeship, some young people we interviewed had already been asked to complete questionnaires and had been visited by the local press and radio. Were they suffering from 'evaluation fatigue'? Our own impression is that they were not. On the contrary, most seemed to enjoy the 'spotlight' and it seemed that the extra attention had encouraged them to reflect more carefully on what they were doing and why. Perhaps what was lost in spontaneity was gained by extended opportunity to think and reflect critically on the path they had chosen.

Where young people did comment on the attention received, it was usually in a humorous, ironic way. For example, one young man, who was training as an apprentice in the steel industry, had 'starred' in an Employment Department promotional video for the modern apprenticeship and was featured on the front of leaflets. He said: 'I'm getting quite good at this now. I know they have to have pictures of us to like show other kids a real face but it's going to be a bit daft if I move on and my picture's still used even if I go and work in a chip shop.'

Another group of apprentices in our study had been interviewed by Sir Ron Dearing as part of his review of 16–19 qualifications in 1995/96. One of the group told us: 'That Sir Ron came round here and wanted to know how we felt about it. I told him, "Sir Ron, you need to get these employers sorted out, it's them that need telling to make sure we get good training". I don't know if he'll do that but he seemed a nice enough bloke.'

Young people who are part of a high-profile scheme, such as the modern apprenticeship in its 'flagship' days, may gain an audience, but usually it is for their promotional potential rather than their critical voice. This news cutting shows one way in which young people were used to promote the modern apprenticeship.

Verdict: It's Brilliant

Throughly modern apprentice: Melissa Attwater didn't want to start her career in debt

When 20-year-old Melissa Attwater, who had a keen interest in engineering, was told that she would do her A levels and go to university, Michael Hatfield writes.

Melissa, however had other ideas. Though she passed four A levels she did not want to go to university "because I didn't want to start my career in debt".

Instead, she took up a Modern Apprenticeship scheme with Kawasaki Precision Machinery in Plymouth and is now training as a mechanical technician, earning £130 a week. She will spend another three years in different sections of the company to obtain an NVQ Level 4, and then work in research and development.

If she succeeds in acquiring the Level 4 the company will fund her university education.

Steve Glover, customer operations manager of the company said: "The company and the training provider have responsibility for the programme, which is focused on specific goals, enables the company to produce apprentices skilled to NVQ Level 3 within three years instead of the previous four, and provides training which suits the company. We will now devote a fourth year to specialisation and contribution towards NVQ Level 4."

For Melissa, her Modern Apprenticeship means: "I go to college once a week and love that because it mixes both the classroom theoretical side and the practical side. Once I have done my certificate the company say they will put me through university, if that is best for both of us. My employer sees us as the future of the company.

"There are so many opportunities at the end of training that it makes me wonder sometimes why everybody isn't doing a Modern Apprenticeship. It has been brilliant. I have no regrets."

Figure 2.1: *Section of an article by Michael Hatfield writing for* The Times *(London) newspaper in 1996.*
Source: 'Return of the Apprentice', Michael Hatfield, © Times Newspapers Limited, 27th February 1996.

The Modern Apprentice of the Year Competition, sponsored by the Mirror Newspaper Group, was launched in 1997. Lucy Pugh, a 19-year-old engineer from south Wales was the first winner, followed, in 1998, by Clare Gaffing, a 21-year-old care assistant from Gateshead. They both won return tickets to New York on Concorde, donated by British Airways. It is interesting that a young woman has won both years running. Lucy's case is perhaps the most interesting as only 3 per cent of apprentices in the engineering sector are female. Their gender would certainly have helped ensure the level of media interest was raised.

Over the period of our research, we came across a number of apprentices who had been approached by local and national media, and by government agencies wanting them to appear in publicity material or to 'tell their story'. The following comments from our questionnaire survey reveal how some young people had become somewhat tired of this 'star' treatment:

> I enjoy being set tasks at work, and working to deadlines. However, I dislike being pressured into talking at conferences, as I have to do another one on the 1st of July (1995), which is not the sort of thing I'm really about!!! [retail]

> Overall I think the modern apprenticeship scheme is very good as you get a whole year's off the job training which is good. But, one bad point is all the publicity I've been getting in the local newspapers. It gets on your nerves a bit! [merchant navy]

Young people's voices

We listened to, recorded, and later mediated young people's views and perspectives because we felt they were perceptive and carried messages for policymakers, practitioners and researchers regarding key areas of education and training. In that sense, we 'used' the young people in the same way as the promoters of the initiatives under review. Christine Griffin (1993, p 9) reminds us that: 'Academic youth research has provided a source of employment, career advancement and kudos for hundreds, if not thousands, of educated adults since the 1880s, when GS Hall was credited with the discovery of adolescence...'

In mitigation, we would argue that we encouraged the young people to talk openly and critically about their experiences, and have sought to present their views in as much detail as possible. By using the privileged access of official evaluators to go well beyond the requirements of our funded brief we were able to spend considerable amounts of time with the young people. This led to lengthy transcripts and, in some cases, discussions in which the young people took over the semi-structured schedule, adding new topics and raising new issues.

Many of the voices reported in this book were recorded during interviews and later transcribed. Inevitably, the transcription ('movement across') from an interview situation to words on the printed page loses the body language, the tone of voice, shared smiles and knowing expressions, and the general context of a group discussion. The transcription process also means that we cannot do justice to the richness of regional differences in expression. The spoken words have been reproduced on the printed page as truly and accurately as possible (within the limitations of our ability to record them). Their expression has not been tidied up or sanitized in any way. We tried to develop a style of interviewing that encouraged the young people to engage in a serious discussion in which we all shared ideas and respected each other's perspectives. In our follow-up study with apprentices, we also played back parts of the tape and showed them transcripts from earlier interviews. This enabled the young people to reflect on their views and take their thinking further.

We wish to emphasize that we viewed the interviewing process in each of the studies discussed here as collaborative, that is, as interviewers we deliberately set out to engage in discussion with our interviewees rather than simply asking questions and recording answers. Kvale (1996, p 226) argues that the:

> ...interview gives no direct access to unadulterated provinces of pure meanings, but is a social production of meanings through linguistic interaction. The interviewer is a co-producer and co-author of the resulting interview text. In this interrational conception the interviewer does not uncover some pre-existing meanings, but supports the interviewees in developing meanings throughout the course of the interview.

Almost all the interview data was collected in group situations with between two and six young people, and all the interviews were carried out in a workplace, training school or college setting. In many cases we conducted the interviews together. We chose to do all our own fieldwork in order to grasp the broader context of the interviews and bring this in to our analysis and discussion.

Our view is that the presence of two interviewers (one male, one female) with a group can have several advantages. It allows one interviewer to listen and concentrate while the other is questioning or probing. With semi-structured interviews (as these were) it allows one interviewer to pursue a line of inquiry that the other may have missed. It also allows one interviewer to keep the other 'in check', for example to watch out for prompting or leading questions; to be wary of 'bees-in-bonnets' brought to the interview; and to be alert to changes of style and tone of the interview. Raised eyebrows, nudges and nods do not appear in interview transcripts but play an important part in signalling how certain questions are being received, activity that can be more easily spotted in group situations when two interviewers are present.

Similarly, we felt that the advantages of interviewing young people in groups outweighed the benefits of talking to individuals. We were keen to ensure, however, that the groups were managed to allow everyone a hearing, to avoid long monologues, and to prevent domination by individuals. In group interviews, people will stimulate each other, correct inaccuracies (useful for the interviewers), and help create a less formal atmosphere that is often difficult to overcome in one-to-one situations.

There are, of course, disadvantages to group interviews. Watts and Ebbutt (1987, p 33) have argued that 'group interviews are of little use in bringing intensely personal issues to the surface'. Some of the participants in our studies might have felt unable to raise issues of personal concern or might have felt inhibited in expressing their views in ways that might incur disapproval or sarcasm from the rest of the group. In response, we would argue that the main focus of our work was to stimulate young people to talk about a range of educational and work-related policies and practices rather than issues of a specifically personal nature. Nevertheless, we have to accept that other stories, of equal value, remain hidden from the research we present here.

Questionnaire data

Some of the data reported in this book was collected from apprentices through a questionnaire survey. This was a requirement of the DfEE, which wished to collect some quantitative data on the apprentices in the pilot year of modern apprenticeship. The questionnaires were sent to every modern apprentice in the pilot scheme, an estimated total of between 900 and 1000. Many of the questions were closed, asking for basic information such as age, gender and qualifications. However, at the end of the questionnaires, space was allowed for respondents to express any view they wished on their experience. Many of these comments are reported here.

One of the issues with this questionnaire, and indeed with any other, concerns the way it is actually administered – how it is handed out, introduced, guided or directed, and collected back. In this case, the questionnaires were distributed by workplace personnel on employers' premises across 14 occupational sectors, and subsequently returned to us by post. Apart from the widely recognized problems with any questionnaire survey, we have no way of knowing if the administrators of the questionnaire tried to influence the apprentices in their responses. We found only one concrete example of administrator interference. This related to a batch of questionnaires completed by apprentices based with one employer. Every apprentice in this group had changed (in their own handwriting) one of the questions to better reflect the employer's policy on apprentice wages. We can only assume that the person administering this batch of questionnaires asked the apprentices to make the alteration. We could not detect any further interference with these questionnaires.

We have indicated in the text where views and comments were written, and again transcribed them verbatim (including the occasional spelling mistake). Written responses can often be just as valuable and perceptive as spoken remarks, even if they are less spontaneous and do not arise out of group discussion. Indeed, being able to put things in writing can often be an advantage for some young people: for example, if they feel embarrassed in speaking out in front of peers or an interviewer; or if they feel more capable of expressing their views in writing rather than speech.

Making selections

In preparing this book, we were faced with an enormous amount of data (qualitative and quantitative). This presented us with the burden of filtering and selecting, from the entire collection, a manageable amount that could be used in a book of this size. Anyone engaged in research, scientist or social scientist, must engage in this task of filtering data and making difficult selections. What frameworks, theories and conceptualizations can be used? In science, the filtering and analysis of data may be dictated by theory. Even observation itself is theory laden in many cases. Where Fleming observed penicillin, the uninitiated might have seen a stunted fungal growth. But equally, much observation and data analysis in science (especially modern science dealing with 'messy' issues such as BSE) is not totally guided by theory.

Our own selection of data from young people's statements has been guided by one major criterion: we have chosen statements that illustrate and illuminate some of the major issues currently of importance to the future of work-related learning. We then organized the statements into the following categories:

- making choices and decisions;
- the academic–vocational divide;
- on- and off-the-job learning;
- situated cognition;
- key skills;
- assessment, supervision and mentoring.

The book has been structured around these themes and issues, each of which is discussed in more detail in its associated chapter.

What can we say with certainty about the statements selected? We do not make claims about their validity, reliability or generalizability. All we can say with certainty (though readers may not believe us) is that someone did say or write them to us, knowing that we might make them public and knowing that any use made of them would be in confidence and with anonymity. As Stronach and Maclure (1997, p 56) argue, 'For the reader, texts can only be authenticated in themselves; the reader has no other resource than the persuasiveness of the text.' The statements of young people presented here may not be generalizable or representative, but we believe they present a range of challenging perspectives for debate (the individuals' real names have not been used).

Continuing the story

As we discussed in Chapter 1, young people tend not to follow the linear progression route mapped out for them by policymakers. They switch pathways and courses, leave home, and move from one part of the country to another. The apprentices we interviewed over a period of five years were no different. For some, their progress on the apprenticeship was aided by being employed in a stable company, whereas for others, the lack of employer support caused problems. Some apprentices changed direction completely by taking up a place at university, and some switched to a different occupational sector. Two apprentices were sacked for theft in the workplace, and one young woman left after becoming pregnant.

Of the 120 we interviewed, just over 50 per cent stayed in the apprenticeship programme they started for at least two years. There were, however, notable differences between the sectors. Of the 14 apprentices in the retail sector, only one completed the full apprenticeship, whereas 11 moved to different companies or to different sectors, and two went to university. In the steel sector, over half of the apprentices in our sample had to leave their apprenticeships. Some, who were made redundant, then left the sector and sought other employment, whereas others were moved by their employer into a different part of the company where an apprenticeship was not deemed necessary. One of the steel apprentices took up a place to study engineering at university after three years of his apprenticeship. In childcare, only two of the 16 apprentices in our sample were still with the programme after two years. Five of the female apprentices had left to enter nursing, four had found jobs in different sectors, one had gone to university, and four stopped replying to our letters. The engineering, chemical, IT and business administration sectors were the most stable, with two-thirds of the apprentices either completing or continuing with their apprenticeship for more than two years.

The DfEE has continued to evaluate the modern apprenticeship programme but only through surveys of a sample of apprentices taken at a single moment in time (for example, see NFER, 1997; BRMB, 1998). They have not funded a much-needed longitudinal study that would help us gain a more in-depth picture of how young people fare on the programme over a sustained period.

3

Young people discuss the academic/vocational divide

Introduction

In choosing to leave school to seek employment or join a government-supported training scheme, young people are seen to place themselves firmly on one side of the English education system's academic/vocational divide (see, inter alia, McCulloch, 1989; Edwards *et al*, 1997; Unwin, 1997; Pring, 1995). Some may have known which side they were on well before they reached school-leaving age. The label 'non-academic' can be acquired early on in a child's school career, sowing seeds in the minds of both child and parents that progress on traditional academic lines may be cut short. In their recent study of teenagers in inner-city and suburban London, Ball *et al* (1999, p 43) echo previous research in the finding that '"choices" made at 16 are decisively shaped, marked and "positioned" by young people's experiences of success and "failure" at school'. As we saw in Chapter 1, the seemingly simple 'map' of post-16 pathways hides significant movement across and within the post-16 routes as young people endeavour to find the right combination of course, institution and workplace (see Wardman and Stevens, 1998; Unwin, 1995). For example, some leave school to start a course in a college and then return to school; some start a training programme and then go to college; some start a job and then switch to a college course.

In their study of young people in further education and sixth-form colleges, Bloomer and Hodkinson (1997, p 84), building on earlier work by Bloomer (1997), show how the 'needs, wants and intentions or, as we would put it, dispositions to knowledge and learning, change over time. For some, what appeared a perfect match in May was inappropriate in October.' Some young people are forced to change direction, as a result, for example, of domestic upheaval, whereas others may find that they were persuaded to take a course that they then discover to be unsuitable. As, to use Bloomer's (1997) concept, a young person's 'learning career' develops, he or she may decide to change direction and hence challenge the neat and rigidly linear pathway model beloved of policymakers.

In their detailed analysis of career decision making among young people who left school to join government-supported training schemes, Hodkinson *et al* (1996) identified a number of 'turning points' which caused the young people in their study to change direction. They use this concept of the 'turning point' to argue against the more deterministic view of the career trajectory that sees people moving clearly and predictably along a chosen pathway. Some 'turning points' are initiated by the young people themselves; others are forced upon them, and others may cause young people to unexpectedly reappraise their situation. This analysis allows room for young people to exert some agency over their lives, whilst still accepting that educational and cultural background play a major part in determining post-16 decisions.

The following extract from a conversation with a group of engineering apprentices, describing how they came to join the modern apprenticeship, illustrates 'turning points' in action:

Clive: Well I first saw the advert in a local newspaper and I was half way through an A-level course, and I was finding the A-levels quite difficult so when I saw this, I applied and I was taken in for a test, and then they accepted me.

Karl: The chances of me getting into university were getting narrower and narrower and I didn't want to waste two years at school just to have to do something else, rather than go on to university. So there's always the chance that I could go on to university when I finish this course.

Kevin: I left school after A-levels, and I was thinking of going to university, and I saw the advert for [name of company] in the paper, applied through the phone, and they said they wanted me to do maths and practical test. Passed that, and then went from there really.

Steve: I was at college doing OND, saw the advert for [name of company] in the paper, asking for apprentices, so I sent a CV off, and they give me, they said come up for an interview, couple of tests, and then I finally got it.

Robert: I saw the ad in the local newspaper before I went in, but before I actually saw it I was working for my dad on the farm, and I left school in July, and so I came here to the tests, and got in.

Luke: I'd just left school, just done a GNVQ in art and design, which I didn't quite finish, I just left school, began to look for a job. The careers office, they told me about the course. I was either going to take a job, or I was going to do an ONC at college full-time. So I decided to take up this course as it was going to employ me as well as doing my ONC.

Mark: I was actually working at the time doing a semi-engineering job, I was reconditioning parts for vehicles in engineering. I really wanted the manufacturing side, and my mum got a leaflet about this modern apprenticeship scheme, and you still have an employer, but still be learning a manufacturing process and all that, so I just went from there.

We have found Hodkinson *et al*'s work useful in listening to and talking with those young people who chose to leave full-time education to become apprentices as part of the modern apprenticeship programme from 1994 onwards. A simplistic reading of their decision to become apprentices might suggest that these young people were not 'academically able' to continue with their full-time studies and/or that they came from backgrounds where getting a job at 16 was seen as the norm. In our research, we found that, for some apprentices, both these reasons were applicable. We also found, however, that for many young people the picture was much more complex. In making their decisions, young people were knitting together an array of perceptions about the worlds of education and work. In this chapter, therefore, we present a number of discussions involving apprentices and ourselves focusing on the following themes:

- choosing between full-time education and the work-based route;
- advice and guidance;
- problems with school.

At the end of the chapter, rather than using this data to further investigate young people's decision making, we use it to turn the spotlight on the education and training systems themselves.

Choosing between full-time education and the work-based route

The apprentices we spoke to seemed to have a very realistic and well-informed understanding of the state of their local labour market. The questionnaire data showed that most apprentices had learned about the modern apprenticeship from sessions with careers officers. The vast majority said they were on the apprenticeship they wanted and that the modern apprenticeship was their first choice of destination. Of the other options considered, a return to full-time education was the most common. A significant number commented that they had considered taking A-levels and/or applying for university.

Some apprentices wrote about how they had been 'put off' joining the apprenticeship and cited their schoolteachers as being the most common negative influences. Parents, however, were cited as having the most positive influence on the decision to join the apprenticeship. Fathers tended to be cited more often than mothers as having had a positive influence on the decision making.

The apprentices were able to extrapolate from the local to the national scene in terms of the general performance of their chosen occupational sector. This sense of labour market realism did not appear to depress the young people but seems to have engendered a pragmatic view of the world of work. The following comments from selected interviews (with apprentices in steel, engineering, IT and retailing) are pertinent here as they reflect the apprentices' realism and pragmatism:

App 1: A lot of places in job advertisements are looking for people with experience in work and in an apprenticeship they give you the education as well as the work experience. I mean if I left for higher college I could do it on a two year course but I wouldn't have any work experience. Well with someone who's done an apprenticeship, they'll be sort of thought of much higher, definitely. [Engineering]

App 2: You get all these people coming from university coming out with degrees and stuff and all the employers are going 'well, where's your work experience then' and the students say 'well, we thought you wanted people with degrees and now you're telling us you don't.' The employers want someone who has got some work experience but is intelligent. This course is better than going to college or university, it must be better to an employer. If I need to do a degree, I'll do one later. [Chemicals]

App 3: I don't think anyone joined this scheme because they thought it was a brilliant job opportunity – it was a 70/30 split between money and training, once you're on it the training gets more important but we all need the money, too. [IT]

App 4: I wanted to be in industry and I knew I'd need some work experience and I knew people who'd done A-levels and degrees and hadn't got jobs. [Retail]

App 5: You do worry sometimes about whether you've made the right choice doing this, like I was on the YT and now I've transferred so I'm thinking, 'Well, this had better work out or else I'm right up the chute but then again, if I've got to go down, I may as well do it in style!' [Steel]

App 6: We all know you've got to get qualifications now. You'd be very lucky to get a good job just by walking in somewhere and falling on a good employer who didn't care about GCSEs and that. You've got stay ahead of the game. [Retail]

One of the more 'humorous' apprentices felt that his future with British Aerospace depended on circumstances beyond his control: 'I'd love to stay on, it just depends on whether world peace is achieved. If it is then I'm out of a job.'

This pragmatism also extended to an understanding by some young people that the modern apprenticeship might simply be an old-style youth training scheme dressed in new clothes. We will hear more of young people's views of the difference between the apprenticeship and YT/YTS in Chapter 3, but the following extract from a conversation with a group of apprentices in the chemical industry is pertinent here:

> Ross: I'd heard that youth training was a bit of a drop out sort of thing, you know, you failed the exams at school, you went on youth training, got money for it and then that was it, and they didn't really train you, you didn't really want to be there, it was just sort of somewhere to go if you failed your exams, that's how I pictured it, to me.

> Joe: I heard about the government being involved and that got me, started up again, wondering if I should go for it cos I wasn't happy about staying at school, and so I thought 'oh they must have changed it, changed YT', and I read a bit, and it seemed like the government had realized it was a bad idea and changed it again, so it seemed to be a really new idea based on the old idea. I'm waiting to see if this is any different.

In the next extract, we hear two more young men, Andrew and Kevin discussing their decisions to become apprentices in the chemical industry in the north-west of England. This apprenticeship is highly selective, offering places to school leavers with a minimum of five GCSEs at grades C and above. The apprentices spend their first year in the training school of a specialist training provider, who manages the modern apprenticeship for a number of large chemical companies. At the end of the first year, the apprentices go through a further selection process to join one of the companies where they spend a further three years working towards a range of qualifications through a mixture of on- and off-the-job training. Some apprentices have the chance to study for an HNC or HND in chemical engineering, over and above the NVQ level 3, which all apprentices must achieve.

> Kevin: Well I tried to get on the apprenticeship when I left school with my GCSEs but I didn't, I couldn't get on. So my second choice was to go and do my A-levels but to be honest with you my heart wasn't in it from the start. So it got to around the March I was due to take my first year exams and I thought I'm going to try again, and I tried again and got in so the A-levels sort of went out the window. But I don't regret it or owt like that. Best thing I ever did as far as I'm concerned.

> Andrew: If it wasn't for this, I mean I don't think I could have done A-levels, I never even started them I came straight from school. Didn't suit me. So I came for this and it's got me what I want for what I want to do in the future. It's not exactly what I thought it would be.

> Int: Why?

> Andrew: ... to be fair I thought it would be totally different. Because coming out of it now I'm in a much better situation than I thought I would be, it's worked out well for me the way it's turned out.

I thought it was... the images of [a multi-national chemical company] all I got was 'they make chemicals' and that. I didn't really understand the way it's structured. I hadn't got a clue about anything like that. Really all I knew is that they were sort of an engineering type sort of company. I thought the training would be sort of things like doing chemical things as well and doing electrical and instruments as they said in the induction and a lot of mechanics... but very little mechanics and mostly electrical and instruments and a bit of process, which we did in training. So to be honest, because I didn't know what to expect, I just thought it would be a good thing to get a foot in and didn't realize what the actual jobs were you would be going for at the end.

I know quite a few of my friends are fairly... well they're not jealous but they're kind of like regretting not trying out for the course because they're all trying to find jobs and things now and there's a few gone off to university and not really enjoying it. I seem to be one of the only ones who's fallen on his feet kind of thing so I'm quite happy.

I got on the second time round. So I was basically determined that I was going to go, if I'd have missed it that year I would have gone again.

Int: So you persevered?

Andrew: I don't think I've wasted a year.

Kevin: I don't regret my year doing A-levels, though, because they have given me a taste of it; you're very looked after and that at school and the year doing A-levels made me realize that it's sort of a big world and all that and I didn't try particularly hard because my heart wasn't in it. So I think that made me even more determined because as far as I was concerned I had wasted a year. So I think I tried three times, four times as hard when I came to try and make up for it.

I don't regret it but I always feel like I've got to make up for that year on the HNC quicker, the way I look at it I've made up six months of that year and I'm going to keep going until I think I've made up my year that I wasted.

Both Andrew and Kevin, like many apprentices we interviewed, had achieved sufficient GCSEs to be accepted on to A-level courses. The following extracts reveal a range of reasons for rejecting A-levels.

Daniel, an apprentice in the steel industry in Yorkshire who had completed and passed 3 A-levels in mathematics, physics and geography with grades that were good enough for him to enter university, said:

Daniel: I'd had enough of school and wanted to get out.

Int: Did you consider applying for higher education?

Daniel: No, I wanted to get out to work. The A-levels were hard, harder than I thought they'd be and I've had enough of that sort of way to learn, this is more what I want, mixture of stuff.

One female engineering apprentice, employed by a car manufacturer in the West Midlands, told us that she rejected A-level Mathematics (despite her impressive GCSE record) in favour of the work-based route. She summed up the views of several apprentices who said they preferred the mode of learning, which the apprenticeship offered:

> I didn't want to do A-level Maths because I knew it would be boring. Now I'm here I love doing the maths because it's car-related. Why can't they teach maths car-related in school, it would be much better, you could understand it and see what it all meant?

The following conversation with two engineering apprentices employed by small manufacturing companies in Hertfordshire continues this theme and further highlights how these young people have begun to distinguish between the modes of learning they have encountered:

> Steve: I did a year of A-levels because my original plan was to go to university but... I wouldn't say I was struggling but they weren't for me basically and so I went for various jobs for apprentices and I dropped out after a year.

> Int: What was wrong with the A-levels then, just didn't enjoy them?

> Steve: I'm sort of contradicting myself here. I left because I didn't like studying and I've spent the last three years studying like hell. But I think the thing is, when I was at A-levels it wasn't for me and I had no motivation. I didn't go upstairs and revise, I didn't do extra work because I felt there was no motivation there but then I got here I thought 'if I don't try hard then I could get into trouble'. I mean an apprentice in my year got the sack because he didn't try at college and so you start motivating yourself. And then once I got my ONC I wanted the HNC because I feel I could better myself, maybe get higher up in the company, and the motivation stemmed from that I think. So, as I say, I left school because I didn't like studying but...

> John: I've never liked school and I always wanted to leave and get a bit more of independence in that you're working earning your own money and stuff. And in the same case as Steve I left school because I disliked it and ended up getting a job where you've got quite a high standard of academic work that you've got to reach.

> Steve: I mean your ONC itself is a couple of A-levels equivalent.

> John: Well then... it was a struggle but I'm glad I've got it. But then I preferred working for an ONC than I would have done working for A-levels because at least it was something in a field that I actually chose to go into.

A number of apprentices had rejected A-levels as an option because of their awareness that some employers preferred to recruit people with work experience. This had also affected some apprentices' attitudes to higher education.

The following extracts, taken from discussions around the country and across the occupational sectors covered in the research, illustrate the importance these young people attached to gaining practical experience in the workplace:

> I did one year of A-levels at college and didn't like it. I wanted a job and money. Thought an apprenticeship would give me most options because of training.

> After one year of A-levels I saw apprenticeship as a better way for me to get qualifications – with it being more practical.

> I wanted to do A-levels at sixth form, but I would have had no money or job after the end of college or sixth form.

> A-levels were advised for me to follow but I wanted work experience as well.

This desire for a combination of gaining qualifications and practical experience was repeated again and again in our conversations with apprentices. The following extract is from a discussion with a group of male steel apprentices:

> Daniel: You get all these people coming from university coming out with degrees and stuff and all the employers are going 'well, where's your work experience then' and the students say 'well, we thought you wanted people with degrees and now you're telling us you don't.' The employers want someone who has got some work experience but is intelligent. This course is better than going to college or university, it must be better to an employer.

> Steve: I'm on this because I can work and go to college. When I started the course I bet this kid £20 who said he was going to college full-time that I'd be better off than him after two years and I won 'cos he's now filling shelves and I'm employed and getting a qualification.

> Paul: It [an apprenticeship] has more of a meaning to my grandparents actually than it does to my parents.

> Terry: When I'd finished the A-levels, I felt, well it's hard to explain, but I felt I'd spent two years feeling like I was working away at something that didn't ever get me going. The teachers said I should go to university but I thought, 'why should I when it's going to be the same'. I think I knew when I did the A-levels that I would have been happier at work. Now I've got what I wanted. I don't feel like I've gone down in the world. I know I can make a go of this 'cos it interests me. It doesn't feel so endless as A-levels did.

Three other factors that emerged were (a) the chance to earn money, (b) the chance to work for a 'big' or 'established' company, and (c) the chance to learn a 'trade'. We have grouped the following extracts from conversations and questionnaires accordingly:

Qualifications, practical experience and money

I wanted to get practical skills and education at the same time.

I wanted to use my education and learn a trade.

I want money and training and good prospects.

I wanted mainly practical work not just theory.

I wanted to have practical qualifications and also have an income.

I wanted qualifications and money at the same time as well as good prospects.

I wanted to be doing something practical and still be getting a qualification.

Because it [the apprenticeship] combines both practical and theory, so what you learn from a book you can put into practice, which gives you experience and qualifications.

Because I wanted a job with training and a skill and qualifications.

Because I learn more from hands-on experience.

I wanted to leave school and get some hands-on education.

Because it allowed me to gain qualifications while being paid for it as well.

Because I can continue my education and get paid at the same time.

I was not totally sure what was going to happen each day, and I am glad that I took the opportunity to do so as I am receiving good training and an education from college that my school couldn't offer me. Plus I am being paid to learn. I prefer the type of training I am getting as it is preparing me for work and it is a lot more interesting. As a group of six of us can be taught easier and individually.

The apprenticeship scheme is very good and enjoyable. The idea of being paid whilst learning at college is great and the workload is manageable and interesting.

The apprenticeship so far has been a hard step up from school yet is fairly enjoyable and varied. It has the advantage of earning money and allows you to do both practical and college work, which makes the training better.

The importance of the company and learning a 'trade'

Because I wanted to be continually trained and educated with a good company.

Because of the offer of good training with a big company and possibility of a job.

I wanted to train with a good company to further my education and gain a good job.

Because you stand a better chance of getting a job and you get training with lots of experience.

Because I wanted to further my education with a company who may offer me a job.

I wanted to learn a trade from an established company.

I wanted to learn a trade and thought this was the best way to go about it.

Wanted to get a trade that I would be able to stick to in the future.

I wanted to get a trade behind me.

To learn a trade, a guaranteed job and the money.

The scheme is a very good opportunity for me to gather practical skills and qualifications and be a more confident person when looking for work.

The best thing about the modern apprenticeship is you get the qualifications you need and also inside experience, which helps a lot.

Training for a job... not just a qualification.

It is what I expected and more. It is immediately obvious that training is undertaken for a job and not just a qualification. Work feels considerably rewarding when its site application can be viewed and the attitude of the training officers is that of dedication and pride which is passed on to students.

So much attention has been given, over the past few years, to the changing nature of the economy, with the shift towards more knowledge-based jobs and the impact of information and other technologies on the contemporary workplace, that it is perhaps surprising to find young people still referring to the desire to 'learn a trade'. The following discussions between apprentices working for a range of small to medium-sized steel processing companies in Sheffield provides a more detailed picture of their thinking on this issue:

Ben: The main point is we all want a trade. We all want to come out of this with a trade.

Int: Why do you want a trade?

Ben: Production workers are like, they are very good at what they do but it's like button pressing if you know what I mean. If you went for an interview somewhere else and they said what have you been doing, I was working such and such a machine at this company, and they might say well that's no good we haven't got a machine like that. If you've got a trade then it's like varied.

Ade: It's universal isn't it.

Colin: If you've got skills then if you've been a fitter you can work on a machine but you can also work in a film factory...

Ben: ... mechanical skills, it's that versatile really.

The discussion then switched to consideration of the apprentices' hopes for the future:

Ben: At the moment I really want to get this apprenticeship, get a trade.

Ade: Make your decisions once you've got it.

Ben: Once you've got that you are fairly flexible, that's our priority I think for all of us.

Int: How do you see the steel industry going?

Ben: Well there's that many rumours.

Colin: A bit more optimistic now than what it was about six months ago. It was really down in the dumps but it seems to be picking up. I think it's like boom and bust. I think it's heading towards a peak again, I think anyway, but long term it could struggle. That's why I believe I need this trade.

Ade: The main priority for all of us is just to, if we can, get this NVQ level 3, get the modern apprenticeship and get training.

Ben: ... you've always got that to fall back on.

Colin: Even if the company does struggle then you've got your trade and qualifications to fall back on.

Clearly, these apprentices reflect the culture and traditions of their occupational sector with its long history of training tradesmen and craftsmen. Their interpretation of the term 'learning a trade' includes gaining qualifications and it is apparent from the extracts above that they have committed themselves to a significant personal investment in terms of time and effort in order to complete their apprenticeship.

Wanting to learn a 'trade' did not necessarily mean, however, that the young people were happy to call themselves 'apprentices'. From our questionnaire survey, just over half of the young people stated categorically that they did not call themselves 'modern apprentices'. Some did use the term 'apprentice' but always preceded by an occupational adjective. Some had rejected the term 'apprentice' altogether. The young people gave the following descriptors when asked how they referred to themselves:

- electrical apprentice;
- electronic apprentice/technician level;
- technical engineer;
- control systems engineering apprentice;multi-skilled technician;
- multi-skilled engineer;
- shepherdess (agricultural sector);
- analyst programmer;
- software developer;
- trainee electrician;
- trainee toolmaker;
- IT trainee;
- chemical trainee;
- apprentice electrician;
- employed admin assistant;
- trainee computer technician;
- mechanical technician;
- management trainee in retailing;
- employee;
- nursery nurse;
- nanny.

One conversation that we recorded between a group of apprentices in the steel industry captures the shifting meaning and relevance of the term 'apprentice' and indicates how young people adapt terminology to suit the occasion:

> Paul: It's OK for us to call it an apprenticeship but if you speak to anyone outside and say you're on a modern apprenticeship, they automatically think you're doing engineering and stuff like that...

> Steve: Yes, they see it as the old way of working, that's all they take it for. Like my dad said, 'Oh I can remember when I was an apprentice doing electrical' and I said 'It's nowt like that, it's different, I'm going for management', so I always call it a management traineeship.

Daniel: If you was in the pub and said you was on a modern apprenticeship people would say you're too stupid to get a real job.

Int: So would you say you were a steel apprentice?

Group: No way!

Steve: We'd say we're going into the steel industry but we're management.

In contrast, in the retail sector, which has no history of apprenticeship and a very recent history of nationally recognized and substantive training, we found young people who were quite happy to call themselves 'retail apprentices', despite the fact that they had previously associated the term with 'builders' and 'labourers':

Julie: I think apprenticeship has a name associated with it, you know you get some sort of training like they do in building, those people who train for a few years, it's associated with that.

Pete: When I told the neighbour to us next door I was an apprentice, he said 'Well you've done well for yourself' and I was surprised at first but I thought, it sounds like apprentice is OK then.

The young people we spoke to in childcare, business administration and IT were much more ambivalent about the term 'apprentice', with some using the term and others rejecting it in favour of 'trainee' or simply saying they worked in the sector. For some the term 'apprentice' was not important, whereas the actual value of the apprenticeship was that it offered a credible alternative to full-time education.

The following comments, taken from the questionnaires, are notable in that they highlight the importance of employment, and for some the actual name of their employer, to young people when identifying themselves in public.

I say, 'I'm employed'. [IT sector]

I'd say I've got a job, or I'm an apprentice (not *modern*!!!). [IT sector]

I just say I work for [name] Travel Agency.

I say engineer at ICI. [Chemicals]

I just say I'm working. [Engineering construction]

I tell people I'm a trainee manager at [name of store]. [Retailing sector]

GNVQs versus the modern apprenticeship

Although advanced GNVQs had become available in England and Wales as an alternative to A-levels from 1992, the apprentices we talked to had not regarded them as an option. When we pursued this, the consensus view seemed to be that GNVQs were regarded as being at a lower level to A-levels and, therefore, not worth considering. This poses interesting and paradoxical questions about the nature and purpose of GNVQs in the post-16 world. Originally announced in the 1991 White Paper, *Education and Training for the 21st Century* (DES/DOE, 1991), GNVQs were intended to provide a broad-based vocational education, including what were then termed 'core skills' (now key skills), from which students could progress into further or higher education, or into employment and training (see Jessup, 1993). Yet, as Spours (1997, pp 66–7) argues, 'GNVQs have suffered from fundamental design, role and function problems due to their uneasy position between the academic and the occupationally-specific tracks.' Thus, GNVQs have had to constantly strive to find a credible niche in the post-16 framework alongside A-levels, which are the preferred entry qualification for university and tend to be more highly rated by employers when recruiting 18 year olds (see Gleeson and Hodkinson, 1995).

GNVQs have proved to be very popular with 16 year olds who do not wish to enter the labour market or seek a training place and who may not feel or be deemed academically able enough to cope with A-levels. They may also be taken up by young people who cannot find a suitable modern apprenticeship or national traineeship due to local labour market conditions. The GNVQs are also very popular with schools and colleges seeking to increase their cohorts of full-time students by marketing GNVQs to those young people who lack the GCSE grades required for A-level entry (see Edwards *et al*, 1997). Our research suggests, however, that where labour market conditions are favourable, GNVQs will be less attractive to young people than the work-based route, which offers the chance to continue studying alongside real work experience and wages.

A further complication for GNVQs and a possible means of strengthening the curriculum of the work-based route will be the current reforms to traditional vocational qualifications. It should be remembered that, despite the introduction of NVQs and GNVQs, some 17,000 vocational qualifications still lie outside the NVQ/GNVQ framework. These qualifications range from single certificates in specific skills such as typing and shorthand, to diplomas in engineering, and many are still offered by the main awarding bodies such as RSA, City and Guilds and Edexcel (formerly BTEC). At the time of writing, the Qualifications and Curriculum Authority (QCA) is reviewing these qualifications with a view to recognizing their potential value in providing the much-needed theoretical underpinning absent from NVQs. If these traditional vocational qualifications regain their place in the post-compulsory education and training marketplace, then GNVQs may find themselves usurped. As we discussed earlier in this chapter, the traditional qualifications, rather than GNVQs, have always been used in some of the modern apprenticeship frameworks to enhance NVQs.

Perspectives on advice and guidance

All the apprentices had been influenced to some extent in their decision making by a range of other actors, each of whom had a particular interest in their future. In the following extracts from interviews and questionnaires, the apprentices discuss the range of advice and guidance they received from teachers, parents and careers officers. The first is taken from a discussion between two apprentices in retailing in Lincolnshire:

> Gary: All our teachers at school told me that I was wrong, and I should go and do A-levels, it would be better.
>
> Int: Did anybody try and put you off, at all?
>
> Kate: Yes, everyone really. Well my careers advisor advised me to stay on doing A-levels, because of my predicted grades, and my parents weren't that keen, because where it was, because I used to live very close to school, so it was so handy to stay on, but no one really, persuaded me to, you know, go for it, but my parents supported me, they'd have preferred me to do A-levels, but you know they supported me with what I wanted to do, so like it's my choice.

The majority of apprentices told us that their schoolteachers had tried to put them off joining the programme. The following conversation between a group of engineering apprentices in Hertfordshire illustrates how some schools give privileged status to full-time academic education:

> Karl: In school we weren't really made aware of all the options that were available, it was like, 'oh, after your GCSEs you can do A-levels', and it's like a big hour talk on A-levels, and then it's like 'you could go to college', half an hour on college, or you could go to a job, full stop.
>
> Paula: They don't tell you enough, it's all by qualifications these days, you've got to have A-levels, you've got to have a degree, and you've no chance if it's a dead end job at 16.
>
> Rob: Yeah, the teachers at school kept saying 'We're in a recession you'll never get a job, and what if you do get a job it won't be a lasting one', they just, I think they discourage us to get jobs when we're at school.
>
> Clive: Now we're proving them all wrong, which is one thing I really like doing, and we're getting paid for it.

Pete: My teacher seemed to lose all interest in me, it was OK when I was trying at A-levels, but when they found out that I didn't really want to go to university, they thought well we won't bother with this one, he shouldn't really be here at all.

John: I think a lot of people maybe want to do the young apprenticeship but don't often get that chance because the schools are leading them down, into the sixth form.

Further extracts, from questionnaires, show the majority of teachers advising against apprenticeship:

My teachers at school thought I should try A-levels. I did, but things didn't work out.

Maths teacher said I should do A-levels and go to university.

He (the teacher) thought I was too good for it and should have done A-levels.

When doing A-levels teachers tried to persuade me to go to university, until they realized when I said no, I meant it, and wasn't going to let any one change my mind that I wanted a job.

Teachers advised me that I would be better off doing A-levels at school. People at school told me to go to college.

The school wanted to keep me in school, despite my best interests.

For some young people, parents and other family members advised against apprenticeship but for differing reasons:

Mother wanted me to do A-levels.

My parents [were against] because I had to move away from home.

My uncle said it was bad money for the work.

Friends, family, because of low wages for long time.

My parents wanted me to complete A-levels and go to university.

Some apprentices, however, had been encouraged by their parents. In the manufacturing sectors, fathers or other male relatives who had been apprentices themselves tended to be encouraging, whereas in IT and retail, mothers had played a part. In the following quotation, a female IT apprentice who was already working for an organization that decided to run the modern apprenticeship shows the importance of parental influence:

46

My mam encouraged me more than anyone, because me mam liked me to do anything like things that educate my brain. My mam said go on you should do it, you should do it, and then I just said yes I might as well because then if I don't want to stay here I can go and look somewhere else.

A group of apprentices in business administration gave a graphic picture of how parents apply gentle pressure to try and persuade their children to grasp opportunities:

Lynn: I saw it in the newspaper and I didn't really take much notice of it but my mum said, 'oh about this job,' and I looked at it and I thought no I don't want that, because I didn't want to do that sort of thing. I wanted to go into the sixth form and do business and finance, but my mum persuaded me to go for it, and I thought well I'm not going to get it anyway, so [laughing] I didn't want it really when I started off. But I only done it, because, just to keep my mum and dad to stop nagging me at first. And then as time went on I thought well it could be all right, and in the end I got it and my mum and dad were really pleased. So it was my mum and dad who encouraged me, they just kept going on and on at me.

Becky: Well I heard about it through the papers as well, I didn't actually see the advertisement but my parents did and they said, 'well are you going to go in for it?' and I said 'I don't fancy it myself', and they said, 'come on, you can make it', so I went for the interview, didn't actually get in straightaway, and I got on the waiting list, and they contacted me, and said I could have a second interview, and basically it was a formal chat with the head of education [at a large finance company].

Stuart: I was looking through the paper and I first spotted it, because I'd been looking for several jobs, and I sort of didn't mind getting involved in business side of the company type of thing, and my dad also sort of works like adminis- trative work, and so he said it would be a good idea, and also your getting a qualifications, as well as your getting money and experience at the work place as well.

Roseanne: I found it in the paper as well, and mainly my mum sort of pushed me into applying and going forward and, and I had the interview at the train- ing centre, then I had the interview at County Hall.

Darren: I read it in the paper as well. It was money definitely pushed me into it, it was me who was trying to stop me from going, but in the end my dad per- suaded me. Nothing really put me off to start with apart from the training centre, it's just what it looked like when I first saw it, was what put me off.

Bev: My aunty tried to put me off, not enough money for what you were doing... but my mum and dad said to me 'as you're a beginner you have to expect a low wage and as you progress then you'll get a hopefully higher wage', and I thought well fair enough.

Currently, all young people are entitled to a careers advice and guidance interview in their last year of compulsory schooling with a careers officer who will normally visit them at school. In addition, they will have received some careers education under the personal and social education (PSE) element of the national curriculum. This is a deeply troubled area. Harris (1997, p 103) explains that the concept of 'careers education' has always been 'contentious and ambiguous' because: 'It is far more political in a direct sense than other educational theories because it is concerned with the relationship between school and life chances; it straddles education and the work transition.'

Personal and social education struggles to gain credibility with many students because it is peripheral to their examined subject-centred curriculum. Careers officers have to try to fit their work into schools whose rationale is dominated by the annual league tables that measure exam results rather than how many children have identified realistic career goals. From April 2001, a new, supposedly 'joined-up' approach to providing young people with advice and guidance comes into operation in England. Despite its avowed intention to raise literacy standards, the Labour government has decided to call the new service 'Connexions'! The remit of this new service will stretch well beyond that of the current careers services:

> The Connexions Service is designed to end the current fragmentation of services through the creation of a network of Personal Advisers drawn from a range of backgrounds. They will take responsibility for ensuring all the needs of a young person are met in an integrated and coherent manner. Personal Advisers' work will range from: ensuring school attendance pre-16; to the provision of information regarding future learning and work opportunities; to more in-depth support in gaining access to education and training and the brokering of access to, plus coordination of, specialist services.
>
> (DfEE, 2000d, p 35)

In addition, the new service will be, in the government's words, 'outcome-driven', which means it will have to meet a set of national and local targets including: reductions in school truancies; reductions in the number of permanent school exclusions; reductions in the number of 13–19-year -old drug users; reductions in the 'propensity' of young people to commit crime; and reductions in teenage pregnancies (DfEE, 2000d, p 34). Hodkinson (1996) has forcefully warned against the technical-rational model of outcomes-based careers education and guidance and the assumption that the way to ensure young people end up as 'square pegs in square holes' is more and better advice. He argues that such an approach ignores 'the cultural complexity of education and training, career decision-making and the transition from school to work' (Hodkinson, 1996, p 136).

Our conversations with young people support Hodkinson's view. Furthermore, we are deeply concerned that the emphasis in the Connexions strategy appears to be on 'saving' those young people who might 'get into trouble'. The evidence from the apprentices quoted above suggests that they, too, need better quality careers advice and guidance to help them balance the views of the various actors who seek to influence them.

Problems with school

In our conversations with apprentices, we asked them to reflect back on their schooling and consider whether any of it was proving to be a useful preparation for the apprenticeship. Most engineers felt that the maths they learnt at school, particularly for GCSE, had been a useful preparation and that the level of maths on the apprenticeship fell somewhere between GCSE and A-level. The following extract from a conversation between engineering apprentices in Hertfordshire, however, illustrates how the apprentices had begun to see a gap opening up between their schoolwork and their current learning:

Susan: I think on the practical side, perhaps in the workshop, I never really did very much when I was doing my GCSEs at school, you know, I mean we were never showed how to use a lathe, so I was quite deficient in that area.

Robert: Did GCSE in technology, I did some work on the lathe, but by the time I'd got here I'd forgotten it all really, so I had to be taught through it all again.

Dave: I hadn't really touched anything we've done so far, apart from maths, basic technical drawing. I think the English is coming in slightly, but it's all in terms of like, mechanical based language, but really not really very well prepared from GCSEs.

Susan: Really from the practical side you don't really do much at school.

Another group was rather more critical and dismissive of school and its attitude to vocational education:

Alex: Well we weren't prepared at school for what we're doing now.

Debbie: Hopeless. Not prepared at all.

Phil: No I think school was preparing you for university, not for work.

James: Totally geared towards university.

Alex: In the sixth form they pushed me towards university for two full years, and I think they were a bit upset when I said no, I'm doing an apprenticeship rather than the university. No not prepared...

James: Schools tend to let you down quite a bit on vocations studies. They try to steer you away from it.

Many young people spoke to us of their dissatisfaction with the final year of compulsory schooling and their struggle to find the most appropriate next step. For example, eight out of a group of 10 childcare apprentices in Cheshire expressed a strong dislike of school and said they preferred to forget all about their school experiences. Generally, apprentices appear troubled by the lack of adequate advice and guidance in their last compulsory year and the presumption expressed by some of their teachers that they should remain in full-time education. The following conversation between engineering manufacture apprentices in the West Midlands crystallizes some of these perceptions:

Jason: You'd think there was nothing else for young kids to do...it's all, 'you've got to stay on, stay on, stay on'. Drove me mad. I wanted to say, 'hang on a minute, I don't want to stay on' but it's like they think you're a bit mental.

Stuart: It's not the careers (officers) fault, they like do their best and keep giving you information but, as Jason said, they always talk about staying at school or going to college first. It's made really clear that you're not taking the best choice if you want to leave. I had loads of arguments with people but they've all been to college and university and that and so they think that's what everyone should do. But it was better for them. Now there's loads of kids going to college but it doesn't mean they'll do as well.

Kate: Why don't they say the apprenticeship is good?

Jason: They never say that. They sort of sell it like it's the left-over tin on the shelf. They make you feel bad about something you want to do and that shouldn't happen.

Terry: The teachers want to fill the schools. You can't blame them, but they end up with loads of tossers who don't want to do GNVQs and crap like that really but they've stayed on because no-one's told them about apprenticeships.

Stuart: We had a careers teacher in our school, and I told him I wanted to do engineering, possibly a job, and he never even mentioned this place.

Tony: I only found out about this place from my careers office, I got nothing about it at school, even though at school I told my careers officer I was into engineering and all that, and he told me nothing about this course.

This group also felt that market forces played a part in the process of advice and information giving and that as a result young people were 'missing out' if they weren't lucky enough to have spotted (say) a newspaper advert or a poster:

Tony: My training providers were really surprised that my school allowed an apprenticeship advertisement to be put up into the school, because it appears, the schools are constantly trying to keep us on for more money, but they allowed an advertisement for an apprenticeship to go up.

Although the apprentices in general knew they wanted to leave school, they also wanted to continue learning and, importantly, seemed to be seeking the chance to demonstrate their full potential. The following quotation from two engineering manufacture apprentices in Devon reflects a desire by young people, who see themselves caught in the middle of the academic-vocational divide, to have the work-based route recognized as a meaningful alternative:

Dave: I wouldn't recommend it to an absolute, complete and utter boffin who gets like straight As in his GCSEs, because that's not what it's about, it's a mix between the two.

Gareth: Yes, it's somewhere between the practical person who, that can do it all, and the, as he said, the boffin, you know that gets the straight As, somewhere like, we're in between there's a gap, good grades, and therefore good at the, you know, doing all the other bits and pieces.

The seemingly interminable debate engaged in by policymakers and academics about the academic-vocational divide is given a fresh and, it must be said, straightforward interpretation here by young people who, whilst acknowledging the difference between the two traditions, want to draw on both to achieve their career goals.

Conclusions

By choosing a work-based route, the young people we interviewed were not rejecting academic study, nor were they embracing a narrowly defined job-related training course. On the contrary, they were seeking a means of continuing their education in such a way as to give equal prominence to their academic and practical abilities. They would also seem to have sound financial backing for choosing a route that can lead to A-level 3 qualification and beyond. Recent research from the London School of Economics has shown that the gap in earnings between people with academic qualifications and those people achieving advanced vocational qualifications (level 3 and above) is significantly narrower than many people have previously realized (see Dearden et al, 2000). In particular, rates of return from vocational qualifications for people starting from a lower level of prior attainment were double those for people starting from a higher baseline. A note of caution does, however, need to be sounded here as the research found that vocational qualifications below level 3 did not realize good rates of return.

Hence, attainment of high passes at GCSE will still produce a higher rate of return than A-level 2 vocational qualification. We would argue that this new evidence suggests that the new foundation apprenticeships should either try to provide opportunities for young people to improve on their GCSE attainment alongside acquiring A-level 2 vocational qualification, and/or it should aim to help as many young people as possible progress swiftly to level 3

These findings deserve serious consideration as they challenge the accepted post-16 hierarchy, which sees full-time education as the most favoured option for 16 year olds, followed by full-time further or higher education. The emphasis of governments in the 1980s and 1990s has been on increasing participation in full-time education to try and match other European countries, but since 1994, the national staying-on rate for 16 year olds in England and Wales has remained stubbornly constant at around 70 per cent. In some areas, notably the north-east and Merseyside, this figure drops to just over 50 per cent.

Since coming to office in May 1997, the New Labour government has begun to address the problem of those young people (around 9 per cent) who do not participate in any form of education, training or employment, and whom it deems to be 'socially excluded' (SEU, 1999). We would argue that as much effort should be made to improve and develop opportunities and provision for the 21 per cent (more in some regions) who are participating in employment and training. Furthermore, we would argue that the young people in our research probably reflect the views of many who only remain in the full-time education route because they cannot find a suitable work-based route in their area. The drop-out figures from full-time courses would suggest that significant numbers of young people are not best suited to full-time education and may have drifted into this route to please parents or to stay with their friends (see Fergusson and Unwin, 1996; Evans *et al*, 1997).

Clearly, there are two major barriers to any expansion of the work-based route: firstly, the reluctance of employers to invest in training; and secondly, the differences in regional economies. The deep-rooted problems of lack of investment in, and commitment to, quality training by UK employers have been well documented (see, inter alia, Keep and Mayhew, 1999; Senker, 1992; Finegold and Soskice, 1988). Research by Campbell *et al* (1999) shows startling regional differences in the rate of job growth for 1991–1996 in England from, for example, a high of 10–11 per cent growth in Buckinghamshire and Surrey to a low of 12–13 per cent decline in Merseyside and Cumbria. In addition to these structural difficulties, young people may also find they are still barred from employment and training by virtue of their ethnic background or by domestic deprivation. Recent research by the Social Exclusion Unit (1999, p 29) found that the participation of young people from deprived neighbourhoods in education, training and employment were affected by:

- second or third-generation unemployment in their families;
- expectations based on past employment patterns (for example, men will do manual work);
- geographic isolation in rural areas and on remote housing estates with poor public transport;
- the expectation that employers avoid people with particular addresses.

Tackling such problems is a daunting prospect and requires direct government intervention. We agree with Evans *et al* (1997, p 11) who argue that:

> If any form of work-based learning is to warrant even the levels of govern-ment expenditure now incurred, longer-term national employment needs must be brought to the fore, with a recognition that society as a whole – not just employers – has a legitimate interest in its accomplishment. Moreover, it is unrealistic and unfair to expect employers to shoulder the burden of effecting it alone. In our view, a state-supported work-based learning programme should be targeted even more widely than at national employment needs, important though they are. Such programmes also have a role to play in helping young people make the transition into adult citizens, and in addressing questions of social justice. Work-based programmes have enormous potential to widen young people's opportunity for learning.

The young people in our research could be said to be the lucky ones in that several had achieved sufficient academic qualifications to be able to choose between the routes on offer and all had managed to secure a place on the modern apprenticeship in an occupational sector of their choosing. They had all, however, considered the routes on offer and decided that the work-based route provided the most appropriate combination of experiences. Their comments, reported above, suggest that young people are continuing to question the perceived wisdom that they should all remain in full-time education, and that they are prepared to seek out alternatives.

In the next chapter, we will see young people discussing the ways in which they learn both on and off the job during their apprenticeship.

4

| Learning on a work-based route |

Introduction

In Chapter 3, we listened to young people discussing the reasons why they had chosen to join the modern apprenticeship, the type of advice and guidance they had received to help them make their decision, and their reflections on their schooling. In this chapter, we hear young people discussing their learning experiences both on and off-the-job as apprentices.

Much has been written from a policy perspective on the various youth training programmes introduced in the United Kingdom since the late 1970s (see, inter alia, Keep, 1992; Lee *et al*, 1990; Unwin, 1997). There is still, however, a surprisingly small number of published accounts of the way in which young people either relate their experiences of learning at work or in part-time, work-related vocational education and training (VET) and/or are observed in such situations. The ethnographic studies of young people in different VET situations (such as care, fashion design, food preparation), undertaken by Inge Bates, stand out here (see Bates, 1991; Bates, 1993; Bates and Dutson, 1995). Bates' work reveals the often bleak landscape that young people inhabit in low-paid, low-status occupational sectors, and highlights how they come to terms with the contradiction between their initial career aspirations and the reality that faces them.

A cross-sectoral study by Gleeson *et al* (1996) of youth training (YT) trainees provides a further valuable account from within the seemingly hidden world of everyday life on a VET programme. In this study, young people speak about the importance of being at work as opposed to remaining in full-time education, with the majority in the sample expressing 'highly positive attitudes toward their training and future prospects' (Gleeson *et al*, 1996, p 607). Gleeson *et al* argue that it is the trainees' 'interest in employment' that has attracted them rather than in 'training per se' and so their overall satisfaction with the scheme is higher if their employment situation is positive (Gleeson *et al*, 1996).

Research that exposes the lived reality of VET initiatives is very important as it provides a necessary balancing perspective to that which comes from a policy perspective. Much of the policy-based research deals with work-based initiatives at the level of overall system design. At the level of implementation, however, the basic model becomes subverted and distorted; sometimes for the better and sometimes for the worse. Much of this has to do with the significant differences between occupational sectors, types of workplace, and the capabilities and predilections of individual employers. In carrying out our own research we found that, to use a theatrical metaphor, there were many different 'performances' of the modern apprenticeship being played out around the country. Although the main building blocks of their programmes were the same, apprentices in engineering, for example, were, in the main, involved in a richer experience than their peers in childcare or information technology. However, some apprentices bucked this trend by virtue of working for an employer who was fully committed to training and whose vision of workplace learning ran counter to the views normally found in their occupational sector.

Another very important reason for increasing the number of qualitative studies of VET initiatives in practice is to counter the way in which young people can be used to 'sell' such initiatives. We saw in Chapter 1 how the modern apprenticeship has spawned its own publicity machine with apprentices appearing in a range of material (such as press releases, publicity leaflets and videos) put out by the DfEE, training providers, NTOs and the careers service. Such material can present a picture of homogeneity across modern apprenticeships that downplays the wide diversity of provision one finds in practice.

As we explained in Chapter 1, the occupational frameworks for modern apprenticeship vary from those that demand minimum outcomes identified by DfEE (target of NVQ level 3 plus Key Skills) to those that include a wider range of vocational qualifications, but diversity of provision is also a result of the significant differences between NVQs. It is possible to achieve some level 3 NVQs almost entirely through on-the-job activity whereas, for others, time must be spent off the job, learning underpinning knowledge that cannot be acquired in everyday workplace situations. Thus engineering apprentices spend the whole of their first year in a college of further education (FE) or in a designated training school. The apprentices we interviewed in the chemical industry were also spending part of their second year on blocks of off-the-job training. In some sectors, one day a week might be spent away from the workplace, whilst in others, virtually all training takes place on the job.

The apprentices in our research were, therefore, experiencing very different combinations of on- and off-the-job training. We sought their views on a range of issues related to their training in order to explore how they articulated their experiences as learners both in and out of the workplace.

Anticipation and fear

In Chapter 3, we heard apprentices discussing the reasons why they had been attracted to a work-based route. Many of them stressed the importance of combining work experience and studying for a qualification, and also talked about their dissatisfaction with learning at school. Some apprentices, however, discussed their initial worries about joining the scheme. The following extracts from questionnaires are illustrative:

> This apprenticeship has picked me up and built my confidence up completely. I was not too happy about starting at first because I didn't believe I had recovered from [illness].

> I feel not as frightened now. First I thought I couldn't cope, that the others could do it all better than me but I'm OK now I've got some mates.

> I was really worried and nearly stopped at home on the first day... I was sure I'd look stupid in front of the others.

> I had to force myself to go. I thought they would laugh at me when I did something wrong but they were really nice.

These comments were initially surprising to us as we know that many young people have part-time jobs whilst they are at school. A study of over 2000 school, college and university students by Lucas and Lammont (1998) found that part-time work has become an accepted part of teenagers' lives, and Huddleston and Unwin (1997) have questioned the extent to which the concept of the full-time student is now misleading given that some teenagers spend as many, if not more, hours working than they do in the classroom. Yet our research suggests that starting a full-time or 'proper' job is not something that young people take lightly. One reason for this could be related to the fact that their part-time experience has been in a very different sector. For example, engineering apprentices might have had part-time jobs in shops and restaurants when they were at school. The following extract from a discussion between apprentices in the retail industry, however, suggests that other factors are at play:

> Fiona: When I started at [name of department store] I was terrified.

> John: Yes, I know, I was too. My mum said it would be OK because it would be just like my Saturday job at [name of city centre sports shop] but it was, well, just different.

> Jane: Yeah, like they do stuff in different ways and the tills are complicated... I thought, please God don't let the till roll run out!

[Group laugh]

John: It's hard to say but I felt like this mattered more so I had to get it right. It just seemed more strange.

Jane: It's weird really, but he's right. I thought this is going to be OK when I first got the job 'cos it'll be like working at [name of grocer's shop] but it's not really... well it is a bit but it's not.

Fiona: Perhaps it's because we knew, like John said, that this matters more, you can't walk out so easily and you've got to show them you're good so they'll spot you.

We recorded a similar discussion between a group of childcare apprentices:

Becky: I'd been babysitting for years, you know my aunty's kids and for my mum's friends but when I got the job at the nursery I was... it's like I hadn't done anything to do with kids before.

Emma: Well I'd worked in lots of places, shops, cafes and that, but the nursery was different... I felt I might make a mess of it.

Becky: Mrs [name of nursery manager] was busy when I started so I like just had to find people to tell me what to do... I knew I looked stupid!

[They laugh.]

Susan: My first day I knocked this paint all over two of the little kids... it was terrible, I nearly ran out.

Emma: You rang me and told me that night, do you remember? You said one of the kids had orange hair!

Susan: God, I was so scared... but I made myself sort it out. I had to, I couldn't leave it like I've done before with jobs.

These discussions suggest that young people elevate full-time work, as opposed to their part-time jobs taken whilst at school or college, on to a higher plane. Moving to full-time work does not, necessarily, mean a simple or straightforward transfer of capability from one workplace to another. They hint, too, that they have approached the apprenticeship with more seriousness than they would a part-time job. This is, of course, to be expected, but that extra seriousness brings with it extra or even new fears of the world of work.

In the extracts above, the apprentices articulate what it feels like to be a 'newcomer' within what Lave and Wenger (1991) have called a 'community of practice' where skilled members of the community are regarded as 'old timers' or even, to use the traditional apprenticeship term, 'masters'. Becoming part of the community is a sophisticated business, requiring patience and attention from the apprentice, who at first is 'peripheral' to the main action:

> To begin with, newcomers' legitimate peripherality provides them with more than an 'observational' lookout post: it crucially involves participation as a way of learning – of both absorbing and being absorbed in – the 'culture of practice'. An extended period of legitimate peripherality provides learners with opportunities to make the culture of practice theirs. From a broadly peripheral perspective, apprentices gradually assemble a general idea of what constitutes the practice of the community. This uneven sketch of the enterprise (available if there is legitimate access) might include who is involved; what they do; what everyday life is like; how masters talk, walk, work, and generally conduct their lives; how people who are not part of the community of practice interact with it; what other learners are doing; and what learners need to learn to become full practitioners. It includes an increasing understanding of how, when, and about what old-timers collaborate, collude, and collide and what they enjoy, dislike, respect, and admire. In particular, it offers exemplars (which are grounds and motivation for learning activity), including masters, finished products, and more advanced apprentices in the process of becoming full practitioners.
>
> (Lave and Wenger, 1991, p 95)

As part of the modern apprenticeship and following the traditions inherent in effective communities of practice as outlined above, employers are required to provide each apprentice with a mentor to provide them with support and guidance and keep a watchful eye on their progress. In Chapter 5, we hear apprentices discussing mentors and mentoring. Our research suggests that, despite the fact that many young people are gaining considerable work experience through part-time jobs whilst at school and college, they do not find the transition into full-time employment an easy one. Their fears and concerns need to be taken seriously and measures put in place to ensure they receive appropriate support, especially in the early days and weeks of starting work. We will return to Lave and Wenger's model in Chapter 5.

One way in which some apprentices find status in their respective communities of practice is in relation to other young people on lower grade training programmes. In our research, some apprentices were working in companies that also recruited young people onto the Youth Training (YT) programme. A group of retail apprentices explained that their managers gave them 'responsibilities' and 'listened to what we say', whereas the YT trainees were treated 'more like ordinary staff'. They continued:

> Abigail: When I was at [name of store] the YTs are just like everybody else, like sales, they didn't get any proper training or anything like I do. The manager would say, 'oh, I'll show you this or whatever, it can go into your folder, what's that', whereas the YTs, I don't think they were following any training path or anything, they were just getting on with their job, which everyone else was doing or sat on a checkout.

Andy: Well, the YTs are treated slightly, I mean we're treated like members of staff in a lot of places and YTs are treated like YTs.

One group of business administration apprentices discussed how they feared that the apprenticeship would be the same as YT, a scheme for which they had little respect:

Lynn: I didn't think it would be very good at all.

Becky: I thought it would be making teas and coffees.

Darren: Yes, totally one sided and you wouldn't be able to like, sort of have a say in what you were going to do, just sort of, well basically given all the bum jobs really. I found it totally different from what I thought it would be.

Stuart: Basically we're guinea pigs on this apprenticeship 'cos it's new. I've got a best friend which is a YT, and he stuck it and he's only got about a month left of it, but he really does sort of like think that some days he can't take anymore.

Darren: I think it's [the apprenticeship] a lot better because I heard people you know, treat you as slaves and that, but in my department, they actually treat me as an individual and they actually rely on me and – I find it alright.

These comments reveal the dangers of having stratified government-supported training programmes in companies that visibly afford greater privileges and care and attention to the higher status group. In the retail case cited above, it was clear that the YT trainees had suffered as a result of the introduction of modern apprenticeship. If the development of the apprenticeship model, split into the two categories of foundation and advanced, is to succeed, then the government will have to monitor the ways in which employers position the two programmes. The retail apprentices had their own message for the policymakers:

Andy: The apprenticeship should be delegated to certain places only because I mean this kind of thing wouldn't be any good in say a single department store where they'd limit you or in a place where people know the training's rubbish or they don't do training.

Abigail: If that happens it will end up like YT, somebody will start taking people without any GCSEs and sacking them after two years and it's not going to do the apprenticeships any good.

Andy: My mum saw it (the modern apprenticeship at the store) in the paper and she said you can apply for this because it's better than YT. I didn't know what it was when I was coming for it, and it was an apprenticeship.

Experiencing 'real' work: theory versus practice

All the apprentices we spoke to emphasized that they wanted their apprenticeship to be dominated by training in practical skills. The following quotations are from answers to an open-ended question at the end of the questionnaire we administered to some 1000 apprentices in England. The question asked them to comment on their overall impressions of the modern apprenticeship some six months into their first year. Here we see how the apprentices prioritize practical activity over theoretical learning:

> The apprenticeship allows practical skills to be learnt that were far in excess of my expectations. I feel this is good as more can be learnt through real experience than from masses of theory. It is backed up by just the right amount of theoretical background knowledge.

> So far the apprenticeship has been as I expected being more practical than academic. I think employers would rather employ someone who knows what they are doing, having experiences as well as having the academic ability.

> I enjoy doing the practical side of things more than theory and at the training centre it is all practical. I think you can learn more from actually doing things by hand than writing it all on paper, and you can also see yourself what you have actually done. I am enjoying it a great deal at the moment and have learnt a lot.

> It is what I expected and I feel that the chance of gaining the practical knowledge as well as theory knowledge is a good mix and opportunity for most young people.

> I like it. I found it hard to understand the written work at first but I feel comfortable with it now – there is a lot more written work than I thought there would be.

> I am enjoying it working on a shop floor and outside much more than I did being at school. I like using practical skills and hope to continue doing so a long time into the future. It's like what I expected it to be.

> So far I have loved every second of this experience. It has been most enjoyable. It has been full of hands-on tasks and the training officers have been extremely helpful by encouraging us to work hard and participate in tasks. I am so glad I am on this course!!

> The boss at work said I'm pretty useful and that made me very pleased. It's different to school, not easier but you get more satisfaction when you see that what you have done is being put into use in the store. I like the college work we do as well but I like to be at work more than at college.

The modern apprenticeship is what I expected. Its been better than school because every one there wants to learn so there is no distractions and I do practical experiments to back up theory.

I expected the modern apprenticeship to be working in the factory for three years while going to college once a week to gain knowledge in the industry. Instead working for the company is a process of learning every trade and all the office work, which is excellent.

In sectors such as engineering, steel and chemicals, where having a grounding in theoretical knowledge is crucial to later application in the workplace, apprentices were conscious that a balance needed to be struck between theory and practice. Here, two apprentices in the chemical industry discuss this problem:

Kevin: I don't think there's anything can prepare you for it in training school... you do a lot of work and things but to be honest with you it doesn't seem that relevant when you come out on site. You spend the first two weeks just walking round like with your eyes wide open because everything's so big and you're just not used to it. That's why we've sort of suggested that people should spend more time on site in the first two years so they become more accustomed to it, they might start to learn a bit quicker then as well. But the third year, I think everybody would probably say it's a massive improvement. I don't know, what do you think, you don't think it's an improvement?

Paul: Yes, I think it's a big improvement but you needed the first two years. Because if you came on site without any knowledge of basic equipment and that... because it's all based around the set instruments they're process-based so that's slightly different from being on site but there's no way I could have just gone on site and started doing jobs on site without my two years training.

In the following extract, three engineering apprentices consider the relationship between their studies at college and the workplace:

Clive: There are certain things you do at college and you think 'why am I doing this because I'm never going to use this in my job' but they tend to try and aim it at later on in your career if you were coming to the end of the year and sort of things and perhaps you would use some of the skills that you've done before.

Int: So what type of things do you do at college that may not be relevant?

Clive: Well you look at some of the science and you think you're never going to use this. Obviously if they set you mathematical trigonometry and stuff like that, yes, we'd use it on certain jobs but the Higher National Certificate is aimed more at people who are going into engineering because on the shop-floor work you just don't need it. All the rest of it, like production planning and control comes in handy because you learn the other side of what people who work upstairs have to do.

Int: What about the thing that Gary was talking about, the connection between what you're learning in different places, has that tied up nicely?

Luke: It has and it hasn't. On some of the stuff it's really good, if someone gives you a problem and then you think, 'oh we've done that in college' you know you can relate it to that then.

Gareth: As far as getting on is concerned, then the on-the-job training's probably the better for us because you're actually… the practical skills, no disrespect to students who come out with A-levels and degrees and all the rest of it but they haven't actually got the hands-on experience, which are needed in a lot of jobs. So doing an apprenticeship gives you that advantage of the fact that you've got both, your hands-on skills and the knowledge.

In Britain, the struggle to find an appropriate balance and connectedness between on- and off-the-job training in apprenticeship programmes is a relatively recent phenomenon. Ryan (1999, p 41) reminds us that, unlike the situation in continental Europe, where apprenticeship is part of the vocational education system, in Britain it is viewed in labour market terms.

Part-time vocational schooling has certainly featured in British apprenticeship, but its role has been belated and partial. Indeed, apprenticeship has traditionally been treated in the United Kingdom as part of industrial relations rather than education. The paradigm of learning embedded in traditional British apprenticeship has been one of job training and work experience, geared to acquiring a trade. The wider educational and personal development implied by apprenticeship as a route to a *Beruf* in Germany or a *profession* in France has been largely absent in the United Kingdom.

However, since the 19th century, when the first Mechanics' Institutes were founded, craft and technician apprentices in Britain have had access to off-the-job training, largely on a day-release basis. Huddleston (1999) notes that the growth of vocational qualifications from bodies such as the City and Guilds of London Institute and from occupationally specific organizations such as the Institute of Meat helped fuel the expansion of college-based courses, such that by 1957, over 400,000 employees were being released to colleges (see also Huddleston and Unwin, 1997). In her landmark study of apprentices, Venables (1974) drew attention to the problems colleges had in relating the theoretical learning of their courses to the apprentices' activities and training in the workplace. More than 20 years later, Huddleston (1999), in her study of apprentices in colleges in the English West Midlands, found the situation to be little changed. Her research does suggest, however, that the closest alignment between college learning and workplace activity occurred where companies had negotiated a 'bespoke' programme for their apprentices. On these programmes, the colleges mapped course and workplace activity to find common learning outcomes and related activities, thereby leading to the design of integrated assignments. Where this had not occurred, apprentices 'simply had to fit in with what was on offer' (Huddleston, 1999, p 185). At the moment, however, there has been no concerted effort by government or the NTOs to push for more integration. Fuller and Unwin (1998, p 164) argue:

> No mechanism is suggested for ensuring that workplace and college-based colleagues collaborate in developing a curriculum, planning its delivery and evaluating the quality of provision. This allows the possibility that on and off-the-job learning remains unintegrated, with providers both at work and college working to discharge narrowly conceived roles and responsibilities.

The following extract from a conversation with a group of business administration apprentices reveals the serious effects this lack of integration can have on young people's confidence:

> Roseanne: I think going to the training centre on a Monday and then you have to go to work the next day, it feels like you're starting again, feels like it's your first day back.

> Bev: I get confused, sort of like, I think the Tuesday's the Monday.

> Darren: Yes, you have to go through the week, building up things and you're getting that little bit more experience, and people are starting to rely on you that little bit more as it comes to Wednesday and Thursday, and they're starting to treat you like an adult – then it comes to Monday and then you're back to square one.

> Roseanne: It starts all over again, you know. When I came into the section I'm in at the moment I was actually taking over a job, which someone had actually got promoted and I was actually taking over a job, and I'm doing that job, and when I come back on a Monday there's work there for me, from the Monday, I come on a Tuesday and the work from Monday is sitting there. So I've got to clear that before I can start on anything on a Tuesday, so it's basically, it's like I've had a day off every week.

From our research, it is clear that there is a well-articulated demand for closer integration of on- and off-the-job training from the apprentices themselves. Guile and Young (1999, p 112), building on the work of Vygotsky (1978) into socio-cultural activity theory, and the work of Lave (1993) and Lave and Wenger (1991) on 'situated learning' and 'communities of practice', have called for apprenticeship to 'be the basis of a more general theory of learning that might link learning at work and learning in classrooms, rather than see them only as distinct contexts with distinct outcomes'. As Huddleston (1999) and Fuller and Unwin (1998) have indicated, however, such developments require radical departures from established pedagogic practices as well as a realization on the part of many employers that the off-the-job component has to be taken seriously.

Adapting to new environments and workplace realities

As we noted earlier in this chapter, apprentices have to learn to adapt to and be aware of the cultural nuances present in the different environments around which their apprenticeship revolves. Through our conversations with the different groups of apprentices, we found that they exhibited many signs of what Engestrom (1996) has called *horizontal development*, a process by which people learn to cross the boundaries between one context and the next. Engestrom distinguishes this process from the process of *vertical development* whereby people learn new knowledge and master skills. Furthermore, Engestrom argues that people engage in horizontal development on a collective as well as an individual level.

In the following extract, three apprentices in the chemicals industry discuss the differences between attending the training school and being in the workplace:

> Colin: I think the main difference between the first two years and the third year was the people you work with. On site you are working with a lot of older people so like it's a more mature environment. I think with [the training provider] it's a little bit more college-based, it's more like classroom work and workshops and all that so... I think it was better on-site, gets you more into a working environment.

> Richard: No disrespect, but I think in my first six months on site I learned more than I had for two years back at (the training school), mainly because I was sort of left on my own to get on with it, learn it myself and there was nobody there to ask if you were stuck. That's the biggest difference I found going on site, you just learn a lot more, a lot quicker and you learn what you need to know not what you're told.

> Adam: I think in the first two years basically you're learning to set you up for this last year. As Rich said, the first six months you get to learn things but now you're still learning occasional new things but mostly it's putting your skills into practice and actually doing the things you've been taught to do. So you're still on that... you haven't got as much responsibility and you're given a wide berth and people help you so you're not in at the deep end, at the same time you get to do the things you were taught to do, which is good. And it does improve your confidence a lot because when I first came on site I wasn't that confident but I'm fine now, quite happy about what I do.

Here, the apprentices have clearly been allowed to put their skills to use and, in Adam's case, the time to settle in. The following extract from an interview with an engineering apprentice highlights how he adapts to take account of the differing expectations of workplace and training centre:

> Paul: On-the-job training's a bit different because there were timescales to meet and things like that but a lot of people have been quite sympathetic and realized that you're still there and they take time out to show you how to do something properly.
>
> Int: How has your on-the-job learning differed from off-the-job learning? Can you put your finger on it?
>
> Paul: Yes. You're not guided as well should I say. On the job you're actually given a job to do and then you do it, to the drawings and you are responsible for finding it, all the drawings and tools and stuff to do the job, whereas maybe at a training centre there's a set job, lots of people have done it before, you can always... you're sort of taken through it.

The apprentices were also aware that part of adapting to the different environments was a realization that each had potentially conflicting goals. The following extract from an engineering apprentice captures this:

> Alan: The thing is you've got the college here and you've got the company there, the college want you to get through, the company want to make money, they're not there as another college. So there's people there that are like... 'I don't want you to do this and write it all up, I want you to get that machine running because that's broken down and it's losing us × amount' and then it's sort of like the bloke at college says 'why haven't you done this, this and this' and you say 'well I can't really do pneumatics because unless the machine breaks down with a pneumatic fault I'm snookered.' I can't say: 'hang on a minute I'm going to take half your pneumatics apart – could I stop your machine please', because that's not how a company works, the company is there to make money.

This comment supports the findings of Brooker and Butler's (1997) Australian research, which indicated that in a context where production is a more important aim than learning, a number of effective learning processes are likely to be underdeveloped and undervalued.

There are other contradictions between the aim of learning and the imperatives of a working company. Another engineering apprentice could not complete one of his NVQ units because of company regulations:

> Andrew: One particularly I remember, it was the hydraulics one. And it says 'take a pump apart, repair the pump, put it back together and test it'. Well we don't do that, the pump's broken – out the door – another one – in there, it's... you know. And I said to my man 'look can I take the pump apart and have a look at it' so I did, but he said 'you can't put it back into production because you need a test certificate for that. If that blows up out there and damages someone I'm responsible.' So it was then shipped out. So what I've

done is completely useless because no one knows if it works or not. So the NVQs really bear no resemblance to the workplace.

Two steel apprentices identified time pressures affecting their attempts to learn new skills in the workplace:

Bob: My company's quite a small firm, probably about 15 people, and I don't get, as I say, no time at work to do anything. Perhaps it's the company's fault but most of my work has to be done at home and that's just the norm at my place. I mean some companies they'll give you an hour or two on a set day.

Andy: Whenever I was... say I was in the canteen doing some log book work and that, sort of it would be a 'how long have you been doing that', 'half an hour'... 'Right get back in the factory'.

These problems were echoed by apprentices in the IT sector where off-the-job training is limited to half a day a week in the company's training centre:

Sally: Everything's done on a Thursday afternoon here.

Joe: I don't think it lasts long enough though, just Thursday afternoon, I mean I generally come in like, sneak in here at 10 o'clock on a Thursday and do some work. We're supposed to only get five hours training.

Int: So you do a bit more time?

Joe: But they like won't give you the time off, we're at work you see, you can't just...

Sarah: It's because it's being done through work, like now I should be at work, you know, working!

Another tension, that of seeming to be 'overtaking' non-apprentice colleagues, was voiced by apprentices in business administration:

Gill: Where I am, one woman, who's been there a few years, doesn't like it when I get to do something new... it's a bit awkward for me as I'm trying to just get on but she's there thinking, I know, that she's missing out.

Anne: It's a bit like that with me only the boss did try and explain it to the others in the office. He told them I might 'overtake' them as I was on the MA... I thought that was a bit off! Luckily they've been OK about it and I think they probably hope I do OK.

Sarah: The older ones want us to do well. It's just a shame they didn't get the chance.

Working and 'being a student' was also felt to be difficult, as these two apprentices in information technology explain:

> Sam: We have to do all the office jobs and then we have to be a student as well, which is really difficult. You're not about when all the libraries are open... if you're working all the week.

> Shaffeq: You're usually too exhausted at the weekends to do anything, you really are and during the week students can have half days off here and there to do their study... we can't.

The following extracts from a conversation with apprentices in business administration take this theme further:

> Lindsey: I think there should be more off the job training, we should get more time for our study, because if we're doing A-level equivalent we can't just have one day.

> Carla: It's impossible to be taught everything, in one day a week, I think anyway.

> Jane: If you think of the people who are like at school, they're there like five days a week.

> Lindsey: Yes.

> Jane: And you know they're learning exactly the same as what we are, the same level that we end up with.

> Carla: We have to do all our work at weekends.

For some apprentices, the difference in the standard of technological equipment between the workplace and the off-the-job site has caused problems, as these apprentices in the chemicals industry explain:

> Andrew: [In part of the workplace] it trains you in the basics but there's only so much they can do because they have only got the older equipment that hasn't been needed. And [the training provider] seems to have like a middle lot of equipment. On site you get really old stuff and really new stuff and none of the stuff that is about in the middle. So you get to learn the basic operations for things but sometimes you come across stuff that's either too old or too new that you haven't seen. Because you know the basic operation you just kind of figure it out and you recognize certain bits and so you do get there. But it certainly helped a lot. It certainly sets your ground rules up.

> Int: I wonder why they have the middle equipment, do you think they look at what's gone on and they sort of go for the middle of the road?

Andrew: It's what they can get hold of.

Ben: Yes, they usually get them off site.

Andrew: Yes, old equipment and that. You see plants have a strip down, new stuff put in and they get the old stuff. They must say 'this is too old, renew this, chuck that out'.

The apprentices we interviewed were very conscious that the biggest barrier they faced in terms of workplace progression was the viability of their employer. During the period of our research, a small number of apprentices (one or two in each sector) changed employer in order to continue their apprenticeship when their jobs were either downgraded or phased out due to employer cutbacks. Some apprentices were worried about completing their apprenticeship as they were aware that their employers were experiencing difficulties. In these cases, the prescribed pattern of on- and off-the-job learning was continuing but within an increasingly pessimistic atmosphere. The following extract from a discussion with retail apprentices captures this:

Stephen: The store is doing OK but if the new store opens out of town then we will be in trouble.

Joe: Our supervisors talk about it all the time and it's hard to get them to bother with us when they're worried all the time about their jobs.

Chris: My dad says I should try and get something else if it gets really bad but that's not easy from where I live. I think I'll just try and complete as much of this as I can.

In childcare, switching from one employer to another seemed to be taken for granted by the apprentices, who were sanguine about working in a sector dominated by very small employers. The following discussion reflects this:

Lorraine: I'm working as a nanny so I could be gone overnight if the woman decides she doesn't like me or the family moves away.

Tina: In my nursery, there's a battle going on between the woman who owns it and the council about... I don't know, something to do with the property or land.

Gill: All I know is, my mum's friend says I could get a job abroad easy if I wanted.

Lorraine: You have to watch them places though.

Gill: Yeah, I know but maybe that's where I'll end up.

Gender issues: being a 'girl on site'

From our questionnaire survey, we discovered that 11.1 per cent of the apprentices in the first year of modern apprenticeship were female, mainly working in childcare, retailing, business administration and information technology. There were a small number of females in engineering manufacture and chemicals. Only 2 per cent of the questionnaire respondents identified themselves as being 'non-white'. By 1999, the proportion of female apprentices stood at 44.9 per cent and those from ethnic minorities at 4.2 per cent. As we noted in Chapter 1, however, examination of the distribution of apprentices reveals that some sectors are entirely populated by white males, whilst others, such as childcare, hairdressing and the travel industry, are dominated by females. The figures for the most populated apprenticeship sectors for the end of March 2000 show that females accounted for the following percentages:

Business administration	80 per cent
Engineering manufacture	3 per cent
Retailing	58 per cent
Hotel and catering	47 per cent
Hairdressing	92 per cent
Motor industry	2 per cent
Construction	1 per cent
Health and social care	89 per cent
Electrical installation engineering	1 per cent
Childcare	97 per cent
Accountancy	59 per cent
Customer services	67 per cent
Travel service	87 per cent
Information technology	25 per cent
Plumbing	1 per cent

(Source: DfEE Trainee Database System, Sheffield: Department for Education and Employment.)

Given that some of the apprentices in our research sample were females working in manufacturing industry, we discussed with them their experiences of life in a traditionally male environment. In the following extract, three young women discuss their experiences of working for chemical engineering companies:

Kate: I think when you start your training it didn't make any difference to me, I mean... people are still quite young, you know a lot of 16 year olds who are just from school and know no different, mostly males. So there is a bit of banter if you like that goes on, none of it ever affected me because I didn't let it. Coming on site I've gone on to a plant where I'm the first female they've put there and... you go into another extreme there, it's different age groups again ranging from there's a lot of young guys in early 20s and then you go to the other end where there's getting like late 50s. So I mean it's quite a mix. But I don't think they really knew what to make of me at first but I've settled in really well and I get on with them. You sort of get the fatherly approach off some of them and the rest are just your mates so it's never been a problem for me. I'm not speaking on behalf of everybody though because I know some people do struggle, or some girls do struggle. I've seemed to settle in OK. If anything it's gone for me.

You sort of get a bit of positive discrimination in a way, which isn't right as well but I'm not complaining.

Annette: To be fair to a few of the girls, there are only certain plants on site that can have girls there? I mean our plant...

Kate: Only because of the facilities. It's fine, I've found no problems at all, quite encouraged. I was dreading site a bit because I thought it wouldn't go down too well but it's gone down better than I expected.

Int: Are there any more women on your site?

Annette: There's a process girl who's from (same training provider), the year above me, is on the process shift team. There's a few engineers, women engineers but I'm the only... there's myself and in my year there's a girl called Joanne who's on the instrument side but apart from me and Joanne there are no instrument females at all I think on site that I have seen. But people have took it better than I expected, I thought people would be a bit funny with me. But everybody takes it quite well, no problems at all.

Int: Have you had any problems being one of the girls?

Lucy: Not really. Whereas at (the training school) I used to get wound up by the lads... 'you're going to get a lot more stick than this on site' and that but I probably got more at college... being on site I've not had anything at all. I was pretty surprised because like I did prepare myself for it and then I got here and it was like... 'hang on a minute, what's going on'.

Lucy also pointed out that the perceptions of parents can be a barrier:

Lucy: My mum and dad are fine about it. They say if that's what I want to do then go for it, they don't have a problem with me doing this... but I know one of my friends, she was considering getting on to something like that and because her dad had worked in industry he'd seen how some girls can get treated and he was like 'no way you're doing that, I'm not letting you do that', which is a bit unfair really.

In complete contrast to the above discussion, the following extract is from a discussion involving the only male apprentice among a group of 18 females in childcare:

Dave: I want to work with children so I know I had to be with girls. My mates are OK about it. It was the employers who were the problem... at first I couldn't get a placement, they think you're weird or something but the place where I am now is great.

Sophie: I think he's dead brave.

Dave: I'm not really. I just wanted to work with children. I suppose it surprised me when I found it was difficult to get an employer to take me – perhaps I was stupid but I hadn't really thought I might be stopped.

In the sectors where the ratio of females to males is more equal (retail and business administration), we found some evidence of gender conflict occurring during the off-the-job training period, although this was very much articulated in the ways one might hear girls and boys at school discussing life in the classroom.

A typical example comes from a conversation with a group of business administration apprentices:

Julie: I think sometimes we work a lot better without the boys.

Sam: Yes we do, because most of them are just really immature.

Julie: They're just crazy, I couldn't stand them in the same room as me when I'm doing my work.

It is as if the 'classroom' environment, whether in a college or training centre, encourages the male apprentices to revert to their school behaviour, whereas in the workplace they exhibit a more mature approach, both to their work and to their female colleagues. Given the rise in interest in the UK in the expansion of the vocational curriculum and concern about disaffection among boys, there is, we believe, interesting research to be done on the role workplace environments might play in fostering boys' motivation to learn and to demonstrate their true capabilities.

We acknowledge that we have limited data on gender issues from which to draw any very meaningful conclusions. The extracts presented above do, however, show that some young men and women are attempting to break through traditional employment barriers to pursue their interests. In a recent longitudinal study of occupational aspirations among 13-to-16-year-old girls and boys in Scotland, Furlong and Biggart (1999, p 33) found that 'ideas about the suitability of occupations are formed at an early stage and overall levels of change are quite small'. In deciding about the 'suitability' of an occupational area, young people were influenced by their social class, educational attainment and area of residence. For young people with 'a high degree of confidence in their likely (educational) attainments, aspirations remain high' (Furlong and Biggart, 1999, p 34). This is interesting in terms of our sample as the female apprentices who had chosen to enter male-dominated sectors had all achieved high grades at GCSE and some had achieved A-levels.

Furlong and Biggart, citing research from the United States by Levine and Zimmerman (1995) also point out, however, that radical aspirations are not necessarily always translated into labour market outcomes. It remains to be seen whether the female engineering apprentices and the lone male in childcare sustain their employment in those sectors.

Rees (1992, p 183) has argued that 'Women's ability to make choices, to a greater or lesser extent, is constrained by the effects of the inter-relationship between capital and patriarchy.' She adds, however, that there are some signs, albeit limited, for optimism in the fact that the labour market 'is experiencing a number of far-reaching changes which challenge the logic of traditional patterns of work organisation and gender segregation on both economic and social justice grounds' (Rees, 1992). The figures for the modern apprenticeship suggest that there is a long way to go before traditional patterns start to really change.

Trade unions and apprenticeship

A striking difference between traditional apprenticeships and the modern apprenticeship programme is the extent to which trade unions are involved. Clarke (1999, p 32) reminds us that 'The history of apprenticeship in any regulated form in the 19th century is... inextricably bound up with the development and strength of the trade unions and collective bargaining.' Given the separation in Britain of apprenticeship from the state regulated education system and the lack of any social partnership between employers and government in relation to vocational training, it was left to trades unions to try and maintain decent standards and conditions for apprentices. In some cases, this led to lengthy apprenticeship terms (for example, seven years in the printing industry) and restricted entry.

As we saw from Ann Widdecombe's statement in Chapter 1, the modern apprenticeship was deliberately set up as a government regulated and employer-led initiative free from the perceived restrictions of the traditional model. Unlike their predecessors, therefore, today's apprentices are unlikely to be initiated into a trade union at the same time as they join the apprenticeship. Many apprentices will be working in non-unionized workplaces and some in sectors where trade unions have only recently gained a foothold.

One of the ways in which the involvement of trade unions might be helpful to the modern apprenticeship is in providing a source of advice and support for young people.

Conclusion

Young people's comments on and conversations about learning at work, as presented in this chapter, shed some light on the benefits and drawbacks of the work-based pathway.

Firstly, many young people are apprehensive about their crossover into work-based learning, just as school pupils often are when they anticipate work experience (Wellington, 1992, and 1993). One talked of 'forcing myself to go'. Even those (the majority) who have experience of part-time, casual jobs express some prior anxiety. Full-time work and work-based learning is seen as 'different', on a higher plane, more serious. It also involves initiation and induction into a new 'community' (Lave and Wenger, 1991) with its own practices and ways of life, and for some this is, understandably, a daunting prospect.

Initial fears about work-based learning were, however, largely unfounded according to the young people in our studies. They clearly valued the practical aspect of learning in the workplace, whilst also being perceptive enough to see the need for linking practice with theory. Their workplace learning was seen as situated or embedded in a real, working context. In contrast, some off-the-job learning was seen as of little value if it did not relate to the workplace. Young people do apply a fairly strict criterion of 'relevance' but often (in our interviews) they apply it in a fair and just way, admitting that occasionally theory is of value and they can sometimes say: 'Oh, we've done that in college.' The literature on situated cognition and the need to embed certain skills, knowledge and understanding in a very specific context, has burgeoned in recent years. Much of our data in this and other chapters shows that young people are aware of both the value and the drawbacks of 'situated cognition', even if none of them ever call it that.

In summary, young people do value learning via a work-based pathway but are also able to identify its problems and tensions. They are able to cross the school/college/work boundaries and develop 'horizontally' (Engestrom, 1996) despite their initial anxieties. They readily adapt to life 'on site' where they learn what 'they need to know, not what they are told'. Indeed, young people are remarkably adaptable to new ways of learning, new forms of assessment, new problems relating to gender, new forms of mentoring, new social interactions and newly experienced pressures in workplace learning. They can, for example, perceive for themselves the ubiquitous tension between the company's imperative to 'make money' and their own need and desire to learn on the job. Young people are realistic enough to see clearly that their own learning programme on a work-based route depends totally on the continued health, success and even survival of the company they find themselves learning and working in.

5

| Making sense of key skills |

Introduction

In this chapter, we explore young people's attitudes to and experiences of key skills. We draw on further data from our modern apprenticeship research and also from the evaluation we carried out of a curriculum initiative in schools and colleges in Cheshire. This latter project, carried out in parallel to our apprenticeship research, enabled us to probe further the impact of key skills on young people in a range of learning situations.

A ubiquitous reference to a set of skills which can be said, at one and the same time, to be *core, generic* and *transferable* has permeated policy documents calling for curriculum reform at both the compulsory and post-compulsory stages for many years. In 1996, the Dearing review of qualifications for 16–19 year olds recommended that these skills should be renamed 'key skills' and, given that this is now the UK government's preferred label, we have adopted this term here (see Dearing, 1996).

Since the late 1970s, there has been interest in key skills in the UK, though their first meaningful manifestation came in 1983 when a set of 103 *core* skills were introduced as part of the vocational curriculum for the new youth training scheme (YTS). As Green (1997) explains, the rationale for core skills was based on the view that the newly unemployed young people who flooded onto the various training schemes designed in response to the economic downturn of the late 1970s lacked basic employability skills. In 1989, the Confederation of British Industry (CBI) further promoted core skills by asserting that all vocational education and training programmes should incorporate them. In the early 1990s the National Council for Vocational Qualifications (NCVQ) identified six areas of *core* skills, which it said could be applied across all five levels of its framework (from basic operative or sub-GCSE level through to degree):

1. communication;
2. application of number;
3. information technology (IT);
4. working with others;

5. improving performance;
6. problem solving.

In 1992, core skills in communication, application of number and IT were made a mandatory part of the new GNVQ. Units in the remaining three core skill areas were also made available. Since then, government commitment to these skills has grown considerably.

The 1997 Labour Party manifesto contained a commitment to 'broaden A-levels and upgrade vocational qualifications underpinned by rigour and key skills' and the current DfEE position is to encourage more 16–19 year olds to develop their key skills to higher levels, including those taking A-levels. From September 2000, a new key skills qualification, covering communication, application of number and information technology (IT), will be available at levels 1–4 and assessed through a portfolio of evidence and a written external examination. A number of HE institutions already recognize, for entry purposes, and/or encourage within their own programmes, the achievement of key skills. The Universities and Colleges Admissions Service (UCAS) is currently revising its tariff system to allocate points to the key skills units for use by students applying to university.

This determination by successive Conservative and Labour governments to raise the profile of key skills has occurred despite considerable criticism from academic researchers who question, firstly, the extent to which such skills can be separated out from context, and, secondly, that the concept of skill transfer can be verified (see, for example, Jonathan, 1987; Wolf and Silver, 1990; Wolf, 1991; and Barrow, 1987). Furthermore, Green (1997, p 100) argues that key skills represent:

> an impoverished form of general education, which is neither adequately delivering the minimum basic skills normally associated with an effective general education, such as verbal articulacy, logical skills and mathematical literacy, nor even attempting to impart a foundation of scientific and humanistic culture adequate to the demands of active citizenship in modern societies.

This echoes Cohen's (1984, p 122) much earlier critique of a precursor to key skills, 'life and social skills', which he saw as a 'compensatory education suitable for "non-academic" children'. Some 15 years later, GNVQ students have to cover key skills whereas they remain optional for A-level students. Given that GNVQs are seen as the easier option for 16–18 year olds, Cohen's concerns are still relevant today.

Green (1997) argues that, in its adherence to key skills, the UK differs from many other developed countries in its assumptions about vocational education. In France, Germany, Japan and Sweden, Green explains, there is an assumption that students need to continue their grounding in general education in order to 'handle abstract knowledge and theory', which is 'seen as part of the analytical capacity that enables students to develop flexible and transferable skills and which will enable them to adapt to new situations and learn new skills as they develop at work' (Green, 1997, pp 92–3). In the UK's approach to vocational education, however, 'General education is only necessary to the extent that it "underpins" competent performance in expected work tasks; it can therefore be reduced to core skills' (Green, 1997, p 93). In her research on modern apprenticeship, Fuller (1996) argued that these deep deficiencies in the United Kingdom's vocational education structures and pedagogies are at the heart of the ensuing problems associated with the assessment and delivery of key skills, problems to which we refer later in this chapter.

Workplaces and key skills

Whilst critics such as Jonathan, Cohen and Green have argued against the United Kingdom's key skills model in terms of its inappropriateness as a vocational curriculum, other researchers have explored the existence and deployment of such skills in the workplace. In their review of research into workplace leaning, Stern and Sommerlad (1999, p 33) adopt the term 'core competencies' and assert:

> The interest in core competencies arises from recognition that the occupational demands of the modern workplace can no longer be met through specialised occupational knowledge and skills alone. Workers within a post-Fordist industrial structure require a set of core skills or competences which do not become outdated and which underpin flexibility, adaptability and transferability.

Rather than seeing these skills as discrete entities, Stern and Sommerlad explain that in some European countries, research has shown the need for a 'more holistic contextualised approach' that emphasizes 'the interdependence between social, methodological, technical and participatory modes of competence' (Stern and Sommerlad, 1999, p 35) These 'core competencies' are then 'seen to underpin the capacity to act in a responsible manner in a complex work environment' in which 'employees are expected to be able to troubleshoot and solve problems; to be prepared for self-directed learning; to be active contributors to dialogue between team members; and to respond quickly to changing work requirements' (Stern and Sommerlad, 1999).

In the United Kingdom, however, the gap between the rhetoric of key skills and employer practice would still seem to be large. In their survey of employers' need for and understanding of key skills (using the current DfEE definitions as listed above), Dench *et al* (1998, p 33) found that demand for such skills was strong, but only if specified at the lowest levels:

The generally low level of autonomy allowed to employees especially in non-managerial roles and in less skilled jobs was a theme emerging from many of our in-depth interviews. Although employers are looking for people who can take responsibility and show independence, in many organisations, efficient delivery is seen in terms of employees working in fairly prescribed ways.

Francis Green (1999), has carried out a recent study of the market value of what he has termed 'generic' skills using the classifications adopted by occupational psychologists, that is: verbal; manual; problem solving and checking; numerical; planning; client communication; horizontal communication, professional communication; computing; autonomy; variety and organized teamworking. He found that, in the current British labour market:

- Computer skills are highly valued, even at 'moderate' levels of complexity.
- Numerical skills have no link with pay (other than by being associated with more complex computer usage).
- Professional communication and problem-solving skills are positively valued.
- Verbal skills carry a pay premium for women.
- Planning, client communication and horizontal communication skills have no independent association with pay.
- Organized teamworking skills attract a pay premium (this was a tentative suggestion).

Green (1999, p 21) concludes that there are 'clear incentives for individuals to acquire computing skills, providing the costs are less than the gross returns' and that 'there is a functioning market for some of the Key skills said to be in increasing demand'. These findings are important in that they are based on an empirical survey of 2,467 employees who have reported on the reality of the status of key skills in the workplace. As Green emphasizes, much more research is needed to track the use of these skills across and within workplaces, both to check the accuracy of the rhetorical advocacy emanating from government and various lobby groups and to monitor the extent to which current definitions are changing and developing.

In the next section of this chapter, we hear from young people in schools and colleges about their experiences of working with key skills.

Personal effectiveness, transferability and the classroom

The data for this section come from a study we carried out of a pack of text-based materials designed by a former secondary headteacher now working for an educational consultancy company based in England. The aim of the pack was to support teachers in schools and colleges who wished to introduce 'core and transferable skills' into their subject-based curriculum. The pack claimed that by developing these skills students could achieve 'personal effectiveness' and so enhance their learning abilities and, ultimately, their employability. Some of the material in the pack was developed by schoolteachers in collaboration with the consultant. At the time of our research, the pack was being used in different parts of the United Kingdom, Germany, Italy, France and the United States of America.

Entitled *Personal Effectiveness Programme Initiative* (PEPI), the materials claim to pull together all the extraneous facets of the national curriculum (such as cross-curricular themes, profiling for the National Record of Achievement) into a 'whole school curriculum model' (PEPI, 1993, preface). By doing this, PEPI:

> ...functions within the National Curriculum to highlight those transferable skills that give the business focus to everyday teaching. The programme strengthens the inter-relationship between form tutor and subject teachers and in many cases raises the importance of personal and social education in the student's mind.
>
> (PEPI, 1993, p 3)

The pack suggests that the materials can be 'simplified' for use in primary and special schools, and 'enhanced' for use in 16–19 settings, including colleges.

The theoretical rationale for PEPI has its roots in the education-industry movement, the RSA's *Education for Capability* initiative (see Burgess, 1986) and the experiential learning theories of David Kolb (see Kolb, 1984). The pack's author claims that, although terminology may differ, there is a general consensus among employers that employees should be able to demonstrate certain key 'skills', 'attributes' or 'competencies' (PEPI, 1993, p 5). For the pack itself, the author has selected eight 'skills' taken from the employee appraisal scheme of one of the commercial companies which sponsored PEPI. The 'skills' are:

● time management;
● organization;
● presentation;
● problem solving and decision making;
● research;
● communication;
● interpersonal;
● self-evaluation.

These 'skills' are to be introduced, one at a time, by teachers through the subject-based curriculum. The pack suggests that each skill could be covered in four to six weeks, during which time students would record how they used the skill in different settings. Teachers are asked to identify the 'business relevance' of the skills and to involve employers as 'partners' in order to maximize 'the mutual benefits to education and business' (PEPI, 1993, p 10).

The list of 'skills' used by PEPI can be mapped onto the current definitions of key skills, and PEPI's pedagogical insistence that the skills be delivered through the subject-centred curriculum also echoes the DfEE's desire for key skills to be 'integrated' rather than taught as separate subjects.

Learning about and using skills

Given PEPI's claims that by developing a range of 'core and transferable' skills, students would improve their 'personal effectiveness' and thereby enhance their learning abilities and employability, we began by asking students for their views on PEPI's usefulness. The following extract is from a discussion with a group of 12- and 13-year-old secondary school students:

Emma: Mostly to help us I think when we get older, like when we get to do jobs and everything, well that's what our teacher tells us anyway.

Int: Which teacher tells you that?

Emma: Our geography teacher.

Int: Your geography teacher?

Tom: And our form tutors.

Int: Did they give you any other reasons?

Jason: To improve on more of education like, when you're doing time management, you can like fit more work in, so you can improve on your education.

Some students (15 year olds in this case) spoke at greater length:

Sam: Already they're starting to help towards our future, I think, because, time management's playing a great part, because we're having to organize revision times for exams. And actually getting to the exams on time, organized, and presented.

Vicky: Yes, presenting our work in the exams can be important as well. Because if they can't read it, it's not going to be very good.

Julie: I think they'll all come in useful at some time or other, because, I mean you always need to be on time, and you always need to be well presented, and you're not going to go through life without coming up against a problem, and you're always going to have to communicate with one another, or you'll get nowhere. So all of them will come in, sort of handy, when we go out into the job world.

Primary school students (aged 10 and 11) also demonstrated that they were aware of which skills were useful for getting a job:

Int: So with these skills like presentation, do you think that could be useful in your job?

Douglas: Yes.

Chris: Yes, neatness, like, say you're applying for a job, like if you make a big mess in the middle, cross out, or spell things wrong, they're going to sling it.

Douglas: They're going to say that's the person they are, oh dear, they're very kind of scruffy people, and they don't do things very well, and they don't spend time on them. They're not the right person for the job so 'Bye bye.'

Int: In what sort of ways might these skills be useful?

Chris: Like how to present yourself, if you go for a job interview and stuff like that.

Douglas: Yes, and like if you're a news reporter and you've got to find out about the person you're doing about or something, because that's research.

Some secondary students (aged 12 and 13), however, were less sure of PEPI's usefulness, though the following transcript suggests that in this case PEPI was seen as just another lesson:

JW: Do you think they'll [the skills] help you get a job when you leave school?

Pete: No

LU: Why don't you think they will?

Pete: Well they're just sheets that you do work from, you just learn stuff from, but they might help you, but if you give them in and say I did this when I was in the first year, and when you leave secondary school they're hardly going to say something...

This student saw PEPI as simply a matter of completing a folder full of sheets. For him the product had taken over from the process.

The following comments illustrate how secondary school students tended to see personal effectiveness skills as having a closer relationship with the humanities rather than sciences:

Int: You think the 'personal effectiveness' work helped you in most of your subjects?

Sue: Most definitely.

Int: Which subjects do you think it's helped most in?

Abigail: English.

Int: English, why is that?

Abigail: Because that's where you use it most; sometimes it comes under geography as well.

Int: Has it helped you in science at all?

Rob: No. We don't do much of that – that's normally copying off the board and practical. And we write in our own words.

Int: Have there been some lessons where you've looked at them [personal skills] more than others?

Sue: RE [religious education].

Abigail: Yes. We used it a lot in that one.

Int: So just take RE; what did you use mostly in RE?

Sue: Research.

Abigail: Presentation of your work.

Rob: Time management, that project we had to do.

Int: So it's come up a lot with RE, different skills?

Student 1: Mostly with the humanity lessons I think.

Int: Humanities lessons?

Sue: Yes, it's mostly them ones.

Abigail: Science, the science wasn't, we couldn't really use it in science, as much as the others.

Int: Why was that, do you think?

Abigail: I don't know it's just...

James: It's a different type of lesson.

Steve: I think, it's more like with English and French where you might be speaking out, during the subject, bringing something out. So it lies more with that.

Similar confusions existed over how students viewed 'skills' as opposed (in our minds) to knowledge, pastimes or interests:

Int: What other skills would you like to do? What would you like to do next? Can you think of anything?

David: Football.

Michael: Kings and queens.

There is also confusion between subject areas and skills. Indeed we would suggest that few of the categories and labels used by teachers to talk about and conceptualize the curriculum are present in the minds of students:

Int: What else might help you in your work, do you think, your school work?

Vicky: Different things.

John: Doing about different subjects, like around the world, might help us, about all the best arguments and people.

Vicky: Geography.

Clare: Modern languages.

Int: Do you think there are any particular *skills* that you could have that would be useful in all subjects? Can you think of any skills that might be useful?

Vicky: Writing skills.

John: Using your brain.

Clare: Reading.

Martin: Concentrating... you don't like just sit there and go 'oh I'm not doing this work it's boring'. You've got to think about it.

This was one student's view of the skill of research: 'Well he tells us a word and we have to go and look it up in the school library, or the town library.'
    One of the most illuminating aspects of the research was the perceptions of 16- and 17-year-old students in a college of further education looking

back on their experiences of learning in their last year at school. This extract comes from a discussion with students who had been using PEPI alongside their A-level courses:

> Int: If you think back to when you were at school, did you do anything in the way of either programmes or lessons where you were developing skills which were outside of your subjects?
>
> Cathy: In science, this teacher made us start making notes, because in first year it's just like dictation... and then towards the end of the year, she made us make notes and things, because we were getting used to what A-levels would be like and that.
>
> Int: Right, and that was the science teacher?
>
> Tina: Yes, it was science, a few subjects, and maths and that was all.
>
> Tracy: Just like basic facts you had to write down and you had to put it in your own words.
>
> Judy: Pre-vocational guidance, we had an hour a week... sort of like filling in forms and that...
>
> Tracy: ... vocational education, that was filling in loads of forms and questionnaires which...
>
> Tina: Some things like with... health watch, then other things like social things.
>
> Judy: We did community service, where we spent like six weeks in an old people's home and then about six weeks in a primary school.
>
> Donna: We had all Wednesday morning to do things like covering wide things, like when you grow up, like marriage and stuff like that, and...
>
> Mark: Just, like smoking and stuff, like that's bad for your health.

Their recollection of specific programmes and lessons, and the names for them, was not always clear. One student coined a whole new phrase – *personal vacational guidance*:

> Tina: I can't remember, you know we didn't do any specific programme, but we did have tutorials. In those, it was just, like deciding what to do at college, you know whether to go to college, and all to do with that... we did do things like how to write a CV, and things like that.
>
> Judy: It was like Wednesday morning, PVG.

Int: PVG?

Judy: Personal vacational guidance…

When the students were specifically discussing PEPI, they seemed to be able to recall specific activities or anecdotes and less able to use the PEPI terminology itself, as the following extract reveals:

Int: Do you know which skill you're going to do next? Have they said what you might be doing?

Tina: Responsibility, about your health.

Clare: Presentation.

Mark: One about animals.

Tina: Pets.

Judy: One about health.

Tina: Behaviour and rules.

Phil: And the other one we did, was if you find like a tenner in the road, and somebody came looking for it after would you keep it or would you give it back to the person.

Int: What was that under, what skill was that under?

Phil: Responsibility [part of decision making].

Int: Losers weepers? [an activity on the PEPI worksheets].

Phil: That's the one! It's about parents and the boys because they were naughty on the bus, to walk, how far was it, about seven miles to school and back, and because their mum wouldn't drive them, and then give you questions about do you think the parents were fair about it.

Perspectives on transferability

The debate over the transfer of learning from one context to another has been prominent for over a century (Bridges, 1993). It was an issue that we attempted to explore with students in the interviews, but they found it very difficult to articulate their understanding of the concept. A commonly held view by the teachers we interviewed was that transfer of skills will only occur if they are 'brought out' and made explicit, perhaps by heightening children's awareness of them, as indicated by these comments from two secondary school teachers:

> All the skills I was doing with the children were merely heightening their self-awareness. It was nothing extra we were doing. But I don't think sometimes the children realize they're doing them, until you make them aware of it. Once they're aware of it, then they do pick up on it throughout, and then that's more effective, in the way that they look at things and try and solve problems. So I haven't personally seen it as putting anything extra in – just heightened awareness of what we were doing anyway.

> We're trying to get them into the language of transferable skills, but not just the language, to actually realize what they can do, and that's one of the hardest things to do.

One teacher felt that students have difficulty in seeing these skills as transferable and identifiable:

> Int: Do the students begin to label these, do they begin to think, 'I am developing my presentation skills', or do they just get on with it?

> Teacher: I would say not, I think they just get their heads down and get stuck into it really.

> Int: So you don't try and bring them out, make it explicit...?

> Teacher: I don't think we've been good at doing that.

It would seem then that transfer cannot be assumed to occur, nor can teachers and curriculum planners assume that a group of transferable skills somehow 'exists'. The label may be useful but probably has little meaning for the recipients.

Previous research has highlighted evidence that shows that students do not conceptualize or recognize the curriculum in the same way as teachers (see, for example, Rudduck, Harris and Wallace, 1994). In particular, those elements of the curriculum that deal with non-subject specific ideas are not necessarily viewed by students in the intended cross-curricular manner. To use a simplistic analogy, whilst teachers and curriculum designers view the curriculum as a well-constructed, well-designed edifice with different categories of building material (skills, knowledge, attitudes and understanding) in a carefully manufactured structure (a weft, a warp, a foundation, a justification), their students see it as a pile of rubble. There is evidence in this study that students do not distinguish clearly between skills and knowledge and there is very little evidence that, in the minds of students, personal skills transfer from one subject area to another or, indeed, that there is such an entity as 'transferable skills'. However, our evidence suggests that transfer of skills from one domain to another is more likely to occur when there is self-awareness that a particular skill is being used or deployed; and when the skill is made explicit, focused upon and highlighted, especially if this is done simultaneously by a number of subject-specific teachers.

In recent years, the number of cross-curricular and non-subject-specific initiatives has rapidly grown, for example: records of achievement, career action planning, personal and social education, careers education and guidance. The ideas and philosophy associated with any new programme need to be cross-referenced with other related existing initiatives in an institution to lessen the potential for confusion in the minds of students, otherwise there is a danger that all these activities will become yet more bricks to add to the pile rather than the mortar that binds the bricks together. The comments made by students when recollecting their past experiences of personal and cross-curricular skills lessons suggest that these lessons become confused in their minds, resulting in a dilution of effectiveness.

The introduction of key skills has enabled (some may say forced) many teachers to engage with the challenges posed by the demand from employers (and perhaps society at large) that students acquire non-subject-specific skills. This has led to the development of creative and stimulating learning opportunities in which students have been asked to look beyond the traditional boundaries of their subject-led curriculum. For some teachers, the PEPI pack simply resonated with views about teaching and learning which they already held and practised, whereas for others it acted as a useful 'catalyst' from which to explore fresh ideas and approaches.

We are uneasy about the language of 'generic skills' and 'transfer', but our own view is that the objective of helping students explore how they might transfer skills is a worthwhile one (as Bridges, 1993, puts it, at least part of what is being put forward under the rhetoric of transferable skills 'should be taken seriously'). The more contentious issue concerns the tactics or strategies for pursuing this aim (see Whitty et al, 1994). Our study suggests that the introduction of a 'package' and the driving force of an external consultant (however charismatic) both raise problems. The role of key staff in introducing curriculum initiatives is crucial but perhaps the two most influential factors are the curriculum itself and the teacher.

Teachers in the United Kingdom now operate within a curriculum dominated by the 'vertical pillars' of subjects and disciplines. The 'horizontal strands' of the Technical and Vocational Educational Initiative (TVEI) years and the now-forgotten cross-curricular dimensions have all but corroded away. The teaching and learning styles adopted by teachers therefore have a vital influence on the extent to which the various strands of 'personal effectiveness' are exploited, focused upon and drawn out in subject-specific lessons. This, in turn, has an effect on students' perceptions of the skills of 'personal effectiveness', which, as we have tried to show, do not match those of curriculum innovators despite good intentions. In short, the active involvement of subject teachers is vital if personal effectiveness skills are to be embedded into the curriculum as a whole, given the current dominance of individual subject disciplines in the national curriculum.

In the secondary schools in our study there was a particular barrier to the promotion of personal effectiveness in the pedagogy found in the traditional subject disciplines, such as science and mathematics. At the college, however, the philosophy of active learning promoted by BTEC and GNVQ had created a far more conducive environment for the achievement and recognition of personal effectiveness than appeared to be the case in the 'A'-level classes, in which traditional didactic modes of teaching dominated.

Apprentices' perspectives on key skills

Most modern apprenticeship frameworks require apprentices to achieve key skills units in communication, application of number and IT, though the level of unit varies across the sectors. In engineering, for example, apprentices are required to achieve the units at level 3, whereas in retailing and hairdressing only level 2 is required. At the time of writing, the NTOs, who design and oversee the modern apprenticeship and national traineeship frameworks, have been told by the DfEE that they must ensure every framework incorporates key skills.

The apprentices we interviewed were all covered by frameworks which required key skills to be achieved as part of the apprenticeship. The evidence they collected of how they were achieving key skills in the workplace and in off-the-job training situations was being compiled in individual portfolios, which would then be assessed by internal and external verifiers. These portfolios can be very weighty documents containing a wide range of paperwork related to the different key skills units. In the main, the apprentices worked on their portfolios during off-the-job training sessions, supported by a tutor who was guiding them through the units, stopping when necessary to provide specific input, particularly in relation to *application of number*.

We present the apprentices' views on key skills under two headings:*usefulness* (to employers, in future life, to them personally); and *collecting evidence* (general issues related to learning about key skills, collecting evidence for the key skills portfolio, and the relationship of key skills activity to the workplace).

Usefulness

In this first extract, a group of steel apprentices discusses the ways in which they might find key skills to be useful. They also explore how key skills can be seen as a progression from the basic skills (literacy and numeracy) they had acquired at school, partly because they are now applying those skills in the workplace. We have deliberately chosen to present an extended extract from the discussion as we believe it illustrates the carefulness with which these young people consider the issues in question and, through dialogue, reflect upon and develop their perspectives. The extract also highlights a major benefit of using group discussions as a research method, as we can see here how the young people stimulate each other's thinking, allowing ideas to flow.

Int: What do you think the purposes of key skills are?

Ade: From doing what we've been doing you can see like it's all like basic skills you need to get on in business.

Ben: Just relating to other people, answering telephones, liaising with company representatives, giving presentations. It teaches you basic skills.

Ade: Having your input... you are not going to sit back and let everyone else do the talk, you have been taught how to put your ideas forward and how important it is.

Int: The ones you've just mentioned sound as though they are mainly communication.

Ade: Communication, yes they are.

Int: Are there any key skills that you've not done?

Ade: We can't really say because to me they are the basics, they are all we need, doing any others I don't really think there'd be any point to them.

Colin: We did think we'd do quite a few more.

Ade: Such as team working, working and relating with others, but we've also covered those units on the NVQ level 2, working with others.

Int: Do you think if you had to rank them, which would be the most important?

Ade: Probably communication, IT and number. We do Maths at college.

Ben: When we left school we like... we were right shy, 'Look at all these adults.' It has helped us to come out of ourselves, and put our own ideas forward so yes it's been really important.

Int: Do you think you develop them at school particularly?

Ade: No not really.

Ben: No because you are talking to people on the same level, you are talking to your school friends you are not really talking to the teachers.

Int: Do you think some of the skills you've covered, key skills, are things that you've perhaps covered before at school? You mentioned IT, is some of it a duplication of what you've done at school?

Ben: There is in IT and application of number because they are really basic, they are like at school but a next stage up to what I did at school really. You go into like more depth meaning and averages and all that like. We just covered a range of things at school.

Int: So you think it's progression on from what you did at school?

Ben: Yes a step up.

Colin: It helps with basics, you can apply it anyway, actually applying maths, its application.

Ade: Instead of saying this is how you do it and that is how you do it, key skills gives you examples of how you can implement it within the workplace, such as collecting data and defining trends. At school we were just like given a set of figures and told do this, do this, produce this. With key skills it says right: 'collect this and this is how you use it.'

Ben: That's beneficial for your business in a way.

Int: What do you think to the language that they are written in?

Ben: Some of the standards are worded a bit funny aren't they?

Ade: Not when you have them explained, when they are explained they are quite simple.

Int: I don't know whether you are aware but one of the things the government wants to do is actually have all post-16 courses, whether it's A-level, GNVQ, NVQ, have key skills as part of it so everybody would do them. Do you think that is a good idea?

Ben: I do now but when we first started we were just given a load of information and we thought: 'what do we need this for we've already got it.' We don't really need it but now I've done it you can really see like we need it. It's like when we left school as I said we were all shy and didn't know what to say but key skills brings you out. It like tells you what to say, well it doesn't tell you what to say but it tells you what type of thing you should be saying.

Ade: I think communication, especially, is an essential that should be an essential part of further education.

Colin: When you go into the workplace you need to be able to communicate with people you are working with.

Ade: Especially going for interview.

The young people in the above discussion were generally positive about the value of key skills, especially when they are embedded or situated in a relevant context like the workplace.

Three engineering apprentices we spoke to from another region were more sceptical about key skills, particularly because their employer appeared less than enthusiastic about the concept and the time spent collecting evidence:

Pete: The employer wasn't really too interested.

Int: The employer?

Pete: Yes, they couldn't really see any benefit in it.

Int: The employer couldn't see any benefit in key skills?

Phil: Well in the recording of key skills. They might be useful later on in life but I'm not too sure... it all depends on what qualifications you're able to get. If somebody was just going to get their national certificate and just be an assembler or a test engineer they might need that actual bit to push them on, give them a bit of credibility. Many people might assume once you've got a degree or something that you are able to communicate.

Pete: Yeah, I'll give them [key skills] the benefit of the doubt for now.

Pete and Phil shared the view of many other apprentices that key skills deserved the 'benefit of the doubt' in that they could see a potential usefulness, but, for the moment, key skills was just another part of the apprenticeship to complete. The following extract from a discussion with apprentices in the chemicals industry illustrates this latter point:

Int: What I really want to get on to for a minute is key skills.

Anjeep: Oh dear.

Int: You can grimace for a minute now!... most people do. Who wants to kick off?

Ross: When I first looked at them I thought 'there's no way I'm going to be able to do this in the time they wanted'. But then I just sort of... it was a Saturday and I just sort of sat down with it and just sort of said 'right, I'm going to do this, this, this and this'. And only after about three or four weekends... I might sound sad by spending my Saturdays doing it but I got it done and out of the way and now it's off my brain. I didn't want to sort of do loads and then start to worry about key skills and doing all this. Just got it behind me now and I'm just waiting for the certificates now.

Collecting evidence

As we noted earlier, the collection of evidence to show one has acquired key skills is a particularly time-consuming process. The paradox that seems to have emerged is that, despite the rhetoric that argues that core and transferable skills can be acquired as an integral part of other learning activities, in practice these skills are often being isolated from the subject-specific part of apprenticeship training, GNVQ courses and other programmes in which they are supposed to be embedded.

This paradox seems to have been created by two main factors. Firstly, the imperative for assessment inevitably increases the isolation of key skills from the primary programme. Assessment tasks are necessarily discrete, or separate, and require evidence extracted from a context in order to be measurable and verfiable. Secondly, the specialist nature of some key skills (certainly IT, and in some contexts, application of number) requires specialist teaching and specialist assessment. These skills, and their assessment, are then inevitably isolated from the primary programme. Both factors act in reducing the embeddedness or situatedness of key skills in a relevant and motivating context.

Here four engineering apprentices discuss the problems of collecting evidence and its separate or 'bolt-on' nature:

> Jason: Well by key skills, I assume you mean all the ones like communication and that. Well we've only just done ours, we weren't given them until the final year of our apprenticeship, this was something that cropped up right at the end and it was like 'oh shit you've got to do this as well'... all of a sudden they threw this core skills thing in at the end. I mean I was reading down through the examples they give and you'd be thinking 'well if I couldn't do that I wouldn't still be working here because I do that every day, why the hell am I trying to produce evidence to show that I've done it when it's obvious that I have'. And we actually end up having a big kick up about that because we didn't think we should have to do them at this late in the day. And we were like 'why are we doing this' like? If it's something that gets introduced earlier on in the apprenticeship and you just do it all the way through and it becomes second nature it's not a problem. So I wouldn't say it's a bad thing but we were a bit cheesed off with the fact we didn't get given it until the last eight months or so.

> James: They're about the only thing that I'd have a moan about really because personally I don't see why you have to communicate well if you're an apprentice, I mean you don't get merited on a job just 'cos you can talk well or whatever. I didn't come for a job because I can talk well – because I can't, it's things like that I disagree with but if you've got to get it done then you've got to do it.

> Simon: Yes, I agree with James because when I came up here they said like 'this is your log book' as in terms of like I do a job, I take notes on it and I record for my own benefit and to claim the skills. But they seem to be making

an enormous fuss of this key skills or core skills or whatever it's called where you like got to communicate in groups and people... and I thought... as far as I'm concerned like I'm here to be doing a job so I need that log book to like... you know, if I've got to go back I need to read up on my notes to do that and with this they were making a fuss of it and I thought... I personally can't see the benefits of it but that's how other people think of it.

James: When you're in full flow of an apprenticeship you've got practical, you've got academic and then you've got your homework as well. So I mean like when you're in full flow you've got a hell of a lot to contend with really and then having another log book again, which is like the core skills, a lot of it is already covered and all you're doing is proving what you've done, where I mean a lot of it's obvious what you've done. Like you are saying, problem solving and things like that, I mean you wouldn't have got through a science exam if you didn't problem-solve. And there's 'show an improvement of learning' as well, I mean your log book going from doing a basic job by the time you're a third and fourth year doing complex jobs, you've proved... A lot of it again, like, all you would have to do is open up your core skills book and just cross-reference things but I mean I think... I don't know if it's necessarily a waste of time but it's just repeating already proved things really...

Int: Do you think they're [key skills] going to be useful to you?

Kevin: Not really.

Ian: Why do you say that?

Kevin: Like the communication, you can't get through life without communicating. I mean problem solving, you do it automatically. All right, if you're an engineer or something you write things down to say that you've done such and such and whatever but just a normal problem you just work it out, you don't need to worry about writing down what you've done and...

Jason: That's right. Finding the evidence for it is the main problem. They will say a lot of stuff is in the book but you tend to think 'well I do that every day', you know, you couldn't get by in this job without doing it so what's the point in us putting down things that it's obvious we are doing.

Int: I suppose the numeracy side you find pretty easy anyway if you're engineers?

Jason: Well that was another one that we had in the fact that we have got ONC and HNC in mathematics and then they're asking us to prove that we can do things like take away fractions and stuff like that, I mean we've done that like, you know. 'I've got an ONC and an HNC in maths and you're asking me to do this.' And that was another big argument we had because what we wanted to do was put in our BTEC certificate and syllabus saying that we'd done it and they weren't happy with that.

One of the ancillary skills which young people seem to develop as a consequence of the key skills assessment imperative is the ability to be alert to evidence as and when it crops up in everyday events and activities:

Ian: What have you done for example with communication skills?

Paul: We were given some sheets if you like and a target of a certain amount of conversations to have within a month, of different styles. Basically you'd go through the day and think, 'I had a conversation here' and make a note of it and you'd fill out a sheet with who it was.

Ian: So it's just a question of keeping evidence really.

Paul: Yes, whoever you spoke to you'd say 'can you sign this and say that... ' I've had a week, a training week, a bit like an adventure training week at college. That was supposed to demonstrate problem solving and you had to stand up and give talks every now and again. So that was quite good, you managed to gain a lot of evidence because it's quite difficult otherwise to try and get a group of people together to talk about a subject.

Conclusion

The evidence from this chapter shows that there are a number of considerable problems with both the practice and philosophy of core or key skills. Firstly, those at the receiving end – the young people – are ambivalent about key skills, to say the least. This was as evident in the body and other non-verbal language during the interviews, as it is in the transcribed words reported above. They are certainly not universally convinced of the vocational significance of key skills, although perhaps the evidence does show that the attitude towards them is slightly more positive in older students. In addition, many young people (certainly those students of school age) make what the Oxford philosopher, Gilbert Ryle, called a 'category mistake' when it comes to reflecting about key skills. Ryle (1949) tells the story of a foreign visitor to Oxford who was shown round all the colleges in the city. At the end of the tour, he enquired, 'But where is the university?' School students see key skills, and indeed many of the cross-curricula initiatives of the past, in a similar way. They perceive them as 'just another thing we have to do'. They do not see the overall structure of a curriculum with its weft and warp, as it was called in the 1970s and later, in the 1980s, in the heyday of the TVEI.

Young people, such as the apprentices, see key skills as something they 'have to get on with'. They learn how to work the system, for example by 'being on the lookout for evidence' or by finding the right people in the workplace to 'sign for it'.

The more general issues, which are problematic for the whole notion of key skills, are also apparent in the data presented in this chapter. The issue of transfer is still an open one, over a century old and still unresolved. It would seem that the 'skill' (if it can be called that) of communication might transfer more readily from one context to another than perhaps IT or application of number. The so-called key skill of problem solving would seem to be the least transferable. Perhaps tellingly, we have no data to confirm this as the young people (and their teachers and trainers) we spoke to had concentrated on the 'big three' of communication, number and IT.

The close relation of transfer to that of the situation or context in which key skills are developed is equally problematic. There are two important tensions here that were picked up in our interviews. Firstly, there is a tension between the need to locate a skill in a particular context in order to make it relevant and more motivating, versus the imperative that it must be assessed. This tension came up in more than one discussion. Secondly, there is a tension between the need for 'situatedness' or 'embeddedness', and the capabilities of teachers and trainers to understand and facilitate such a process. Key skills such as IT or application of number often require specialist input. In practice, therefore, their 'delivery' is extracted from the everyday or workplace situation. This is especially obvious in the case of IT, which required a separate, dedicated teaching space, often on a different site or in a different part of the school, college or training centre. In short, situatedness is not easy to attain due to the demands of assessment and the need for specialist input.

We feel that by listening to young people discuss key skills, we have improved our understanding of their difficulties and their potential value.

6

Mentors and mentoring, supervisors and supervision, assessors and assessment in the workplace

Introduction

In this chapter, we present young people's experiences of being 'mentored', 'supervised', 'trained', and assessed in the workplace. Their perspectives reveal a disturbing picture of the contemporary workplace in which young people are often left to fend for themselves and struggling to get the level of training they need and deserve.

A key role in any modern apprentice programme is that of the 'mentor', more experienced employees who, like the supervisor of old, take the younger workers under their wings and be there to advise, listen, and explain as and when necessary. The need for mentors was argued to be significant given that the modern apprenticeship was introducing young people, often straight from school, into complex working environments where they would be expected to train for an NVQ level 3 and, in some cases, other qualification, develop a range of key skills, cope with on- and off-the-job training; cope with different assessment regimes; and, perhaps, cope with employers who were themselves new to the demands and requirements of substantive training programmes (see QPID, 2000).

The concept of the mentor has, of course, been around for a long time. The original Mentor was appointed by Ulysses to be tutor and advisor to his son. Since then the role has taken a range of forms along a continuum from someone who merely looks after another person (student or colleague) in a general sense to someone who systematically passes on their expertise to another, as in the traditional master–apprentice or expert–novice relationship. Mentors can, therefore, be colleagues who combine their mentoring role with one or more of the following roles, or, indeed, colleagues who define their mentoring role as being one or more of the following:

- trainer;
- supervisor;

- coach;
- advisor;
- counsellor;
- critical friend.

Recent literature on workplace learning has started to use the term 'key worker' to denote someone who can 'coach, help and support other workers and create a climate favourable to learning in which people seek advice and help from each other' (NSTF, 2000, p 37; see also Stern and Sommerlad, 1999).

The use of mentors has become common in many occupational sectors and in professional education programmes. They are a central feature of the teacher training system in England and Wales in which trainees are assigned a more experienced teacher as their mentor whilst on teaching practice (see Dunne and Bennett, 1997; and Blake *et al*, 1998). Unemployed people on the New Deal programme are also assigned a mentor during the period they spend in the 'learning gateway', although here the role is firmly at the advisory end of the continuum.

Determining what a mentor does will largely depend on the nature of the learning setting (be that a workplace, school, college and so forth), and the number of experienced people available. As far as workplace settings go, Stern and Sommerlad (1999, p 61) remind us that, 'Many companies lack the types of sophisticated personnel management systems necessary to make effective training and utilisation of workers' abilities a reality.' This view may, of course, also reflect the situation in many educational establishments. A mentor may find that he or she has not been allocated enough time to carry out duties properly or that mentoring conflicts with one of his or her other roles: for example, if a mentor is also a line manager or an in-house assessor. In their study of mentors in the modern apprenticeship, QPID (2000, p 5) found that 'Every apprentice has a variety of people who are responsible for some aspect of their training or supervision – tutors, assessors, line managers, training advisors, etc' but they assert that what makes 'true mentoring distinctive' is:

> its ability to take into account all aspects of the apprentice as an individual, to take a long term view of the needs and potential of the apprentice, and to be independent of the requirements to impose discipline or make judgements (which are key components of other roles).
>
> (QPID, 2000, p 5)

Expressed in this way, the role of the mentor takes on a guardian angel dimension. It is perhaps not surprising, then, that the same report concluded that the concept of mentoring in the modern apprenticeship 'appeared to be poorly understood' (QPID, 2000, p 7).

Learning at work

As the QPID (2000) report highlighted, apprentices and young workers more generally will encounter several people in the workplace to whom they will need to look for advice and expertise. Historically, apprentices were expected to learn their craft or trade by 'sitting by Nellie', which involved watching experienced workers and then attempting to replicate their skills by producing a 'practice piece'; this could be a cabinet or particular form of tool or machine part (cf. the concept/metaphor of 'scaffolding' learning). Lane (1996, p 76), writing about apprenticeship in England prior to the establishment of technical institutes at the end of the 19th century, explains that:

> Exactly how an apprentice was taught varied considerably even within one occupation, for curricula did not exist; however, there was in all skills a corpus of knowledge to which each master would add his own 'tricks' and personal innovations.

Many apprentices today will not, of course, be training to make things or indeed be training for a specific trade or craft. The growth of the service sector and the decline of manufacturing have reduced the numbers of apprentices in traditional sectors considerably. Apprentices at the start of the 21st century are more likely to be training to sell than make, and will certainly be required to retrain at various points in their working life.

In the contemporary workplace, therefore, an apprentice is unlikely to be assigned to a 'master' in the traditional sense but will learn the skills and knowledge of the sectors they are in from a number of people in the workplace, as well as through attending off-the-job training at a college or training centre. However, a major problem for apprenticeship, and workplace learning more generally, in the UK, is that the quality of on-the-job training is extremely variable. Keep (1999) links this to a broader critique of systemic problems in the organization, vision and goals of industry and commerce in the UK, which he argues still reflect those of the 19th rather than the 21st century. Thus too many employers are content with producing low-quality products or delivering poor services. This results in employers recruiting people with low skills to whom the minimum amount of training is given, and who have little chance of exercising any autonomy in the workplace. Keep (1999, p 336) argues that:

> A traditional reliance on managers to undertake the thinking, planning, design and decision making elements of work, while the non-managerial workforce gets on with following procedures and taking orders, would appear to still be the norm.

Other studies have shown that employers do take training seriously but only when they are required to comply with statutory regulations as in, for example, the Health and Safety Act, the Food Safety Act, and the Control of Substances Hazardous to Health Regulations Act (see Felstead and Green, 1996).

In addition to employer reluctance to offer training above and beyond the minimum required to perform a narrow set of functions, there is still no requirement in the UK for workplace trainers to be trained. This situation was supposed to be addressed when the competence-based national vocational qualifications (NVQs) were first introduced in the late 1980s. National vocational qualifications were originally designed to be wholly achieved in the workplace. Employees were to be assessed by colleagues who themselves were trained trainers and trained in assessment. In addition, more senior people in the workplace would take on the role of an 'internal verifier' and they, too, would be trained. Gilbert Jessup, the chief architect of the competence-based model, argued that the assessor must be someone in daily contact with the person being assessed. He said:

> The potential benefits of making supervisors and managers responsible for assessment and continuing learning are considerable. A consciousness of the standards required in their employment area relates closely to their primary role of maintaining standards of performance and quality of products and services in their company. It provides a framework and a language to discuss improving their company standards and the quality of their products.
>
> (Jessup, 1991, p 52)

The competence-based model has been severely criticized and it is not our intention here to revisit those criticisms (see, inter alia, Hyland, 1994; Hodkinson and Issitt, 1995; Wolf, 1995; Raggatt and Williams, 2000). It is important simply to note that Jessup's vision has not materialized. Many employers rejected the competence model, and hence NVQs, because, as a host of academic critics have pointed out, this approach reduces skill acquisition to a list of simplistic and decontextualized behavioural tasks. At level 1, which covers basic routine tasks, the approach is possibly acceptable, but beyond that it is inadequate. Employers also failed to rush to embrace NVQs because they found the emphasis on workplace assessment to be unrealistic. Their staff were too busy doing their proper jobs to have the time to carry out a function traditionally seen as the preserve of colleges and other training providers. Some employers have welcomed NVQs as vehicles for assessing, and therefore recognizing, (generally mature) employees' existing competence in order to identify training needs. Unwin (1991) also found evidence of a chemical company using NVQs to recognize the skills of process operators in order to introduce a new reward system. In the main, however, the model appears to be deeply flawed and has not led to any meaningful improvement in training standards in British workplaces.

Despite the well-documented problems with NVQs, however, both pre-vious Tory and now the current Labour government have retained these qualifications and made them the goal for all government-supported train-ing programmes including the modern apprenticeship. As we noted in Chapter 2, apprentices are required to train to NVQ level 3. This means that a great deal of assessment must occur in the workplace. In this chap-ter we reveal how apprentices in a range of settings experience workplace assessment.

Those apprentices (for example in engineering, chemicals and steel) who are also studying for traditional vocational qualifications encounter other forms of assessment through, for example, oral and written examinations, assignments and projects. In addition, as we saw in Chapter 4, all appren-tices have to be assessed against the key skills criteria. All in all, during their apprenticeship the young people to whom we spoke were encountering a great deal of assessment.

The rest of this chapter, in which we hear from young people, is divided into two sections: mentors and supervisors; and assessors and assessment.

Mentors and supervisors

In the following conversation, three engineering apprentices in a large car manufacturing plant discuss their relationship with mentors and super-visors.

Int: How do you decide who to ask for help or advise and how do you go about it?

Chris: At first you are a bit nervous to approach them aren't you, you think they've got a lot on their plate and you are going to ask them about this thing and really they are too short of time.

Barbara: I aim to ask supervisors rather than normal shop floor blokes because they are used to like helping you out with signing stuff for the NVQ.

Andy: You go to people who you feel comfortable about actually asking them things and they'll say something positive.

Int: Has anybody ever refused to help, or given you the impression they don't want to?

Barbara: No not really I've never had that. I don't know whether the others have.

Chris: Sometimes you get a bit of mickey taken like but they don't say no…

Andy: Yeah, they say stuff like 'teaching you to suck eggs'. I think, when we go to them for some assessment, they wonder why they've got to sign something, say like for a discussion for key skills, that they've just had with you if you know what I mean.

Int: Do you have a particular person in your workplace who you'd call your mentor?

Chris: We did have but he were made redundant weren't he.

Barbara: Yeah, the company is in a bit of trouble at the minute so they've been laying a lot of blokes off. There's a training officer but it's quite hard to get hold of him and another one's been laid off.

Andy: In terms of actual mentors, where someone is appointed for us to deal with, like a shopfloor worker, a maintenance fitter, well we'll go round with him, we'll follow him round.

Barbara: They are really our mentors at the minute. Our manager also knows who we are. They don't call themselves that but we have to get help from anyone really so if you're told to work with someone like, as Andy said, a fitter, then you treat him as your mentor, even if it's only for a week or two. Then there's workers on different parts of the plant that you don't come into contact with a lot. You might go out on a job in their particular area and they might assist you or you might assist them. They wouldn't really be responsible for you but you may work with them.

Andy: At the minute we are not stationed in one position, every six months we will move round, so we have to get to know a different set of blokes and who we can ask and who we can't ask.

Barbara: In a way they know they are mentors because they were apprentices when they were young and they know it's that you work with a bloke and he teaches you the job so they do exactly the same as what happened to them when they were younger, so yes they do.

Int: Would they use that term – mentor? What would they call themselves?

Andy: Gaffer!

Int: But nobody walks round with a big badge saying 'mentor'?

Andy: Not really.

Chris: There was one... our top mentor sort of thing. He'd do our assessment, but he was made redundant. But then, it's sort of more divided isn't it, separate working divisions with some people doing assessment and some supposed to be mentoring, and then there's the managers so it's all a bit confusing. You end up talking mainly to the bloke you're working with that day.

Int: Before this person was made redundant, was it useful to have a person like that?

Barbara: It was because any question we'd got we'd just go to ask him, but now as I say we don't know who really should do this. It's been turned upside down.

Int: You can learn a lot from people who aren't sort of a regular mentor?

Barbara: Definitely, in fact they are the only people we've been learning from. Him that got laid off, he was sat in an office and we got put with different blokes and they're the only people who we are learning things off, that's who we are learning our trade from, from the actual workers not from the mentors.

Chris: It's not just a problem that the mentor bloke was made redundant, but there has been quite a big shift in the company, like the whole structure has changed so that has affected our NVQ. The personnel department has got pushed to the background sort of thing.

Int: It has affected the NVQ because there is nobody to assess you?

Barbara: There is nobody to assess us on the job. Well, I think it's that there's nobody like in charge of it. We are actually having to pursue it ourselves and say 'have you sorted anything out', whereas before it would be all laid out. It's up in arms really. We were like guinea pigs really, if you can call us that.

These apprentices show the gap between the policy requirement that all apprentices should have a 'named' mentor and the reality in the workplace. This group, at least, was fortunate in that it worked in a large company employing many apprentices who look to each other for support. Many apprentices are, however, much more isolated. The next discussion, between a group of apprentices working in the childcare sector, presents a set of problems different from those facing the engineers. These apprentices were interviewed as a group at their training provider premises, which they attend one day per week. They were all working for different sorts and sizes of employer (in public and private nurseries, and in private homes as nannies) spread throughout Cheshire.

Sally: In our nursery, there's Sue the boss, and then there's three nursery nurses who trained in college so I'm the only one on modern apprenticeship. Sue said she was my mentor when I started but she's very busy. Tina is supposed to do my assessing. I'm better now than I was... I used to not like to ask anything. The best person I think is Ann here at [name of training provider], 'cos she knows us best and she's dead nice.

Jenny: Well I'm a nanny for two little boys. The mum works so I'm on my own all day. She's knackered when she comes home but she tries to listen. Funny really, as she probably knows less than me because she hasn't done a course, she like just had them but I'm the one who's looking after them!

[Everyone laughs.]

Nicola: I agree with Sally that it's Ann who we would say was our mentor because, well, for one reason she understands what we're doing on the apprenticeship. Where I work [in a large council-run day nursery] everyone's OK with me and shows me how to do things but I wouldn't tell them I was worried about something or if I had a problem. No, I'd talk to Ann.

Here the apprentices' relationship with their off-the-job trainer appears to be much more significant than any they currently have with their colleagues in the workplace.

A different picture again was presented by a group of retail apprentices working in a department store in a city centre. They were located in various sections of the store (china, clothing, electrical goods) and attended off-the-job training one day per week in the company's training centre.

Douglas: We've got a mentor who is the personnel manager and we can go to her if we've got any problems. I'd say, I don't know what the others think, that she's OK and seems to listen.

Jane: Yes, I'd agree.

Pete: The problem is that she's very busy. And what if she left and the new person wasn't as nice?

Emma: We have to get on with everyone really, that's what I've learned. You can't afford to get on the wrong side of people. We need to talk to each other too, as we're all in the same position, the same boat. It's like we need to stick together...

Imran: She's right. The mentor thing is about making sure we do our job and attend training. I know she listens but if we had a real problem, say someone was picking on us, then it could be a problem knowing who to tell.

Jane: I talk to my mum – perhaps they should pay her to be my mentor!

The extracts above suggest that apprentices are likely to meet a whole panoply of people who might have a role to play in their training and development but that it is somewhat ad hoc as to how much time they will spend with a supervisor or mentor who has been properly trained in that role. Many of these people will probably have something useful to impart but Eraut points out the dangers of relying too much on everyday experience:

Untrained mentors are likely to show rather than explain, and may even have difficulty in providing an appropriate explanation because they have become so immersed in the taken-for-granted world of that particular work-context.

(Eraut, 1994, p 209)

Pillay *et al* (1998), however, suggest that too much reliance on 'experts' can encourage the learner to become too dependent:

> In workplace learning environments, individuals who believe knowledge is transmitted from an expert to a novice, may not seek knowledge by asking questions and experimenting with alternatives. This raises issues about the process of mentoring where learners are expected to quiz the mentor and model their thoughts and actions. These learners would prefer to be told and shown procedures where they just absorb the information with limited or no cognitive engagement. Conversely, trainees who believe that knowledge is personally constructed and not simply absorbed, are more likely to engage in active construction of knowledge.
>
> (Pillay *et al*, 1998, p 242)

We would argue that supervision and mentoring on the modern apprenticeship are still crudely defined, leaving young people in vulnerable positions. Mentoring is haphazard and unpredictable. The apprentices we spoke to expressed anxiety about their confusion as to who they should regard as a mentor, and to whom they should look for 'expert' knowledge and understanding when it came to learning a new job function. They may have been, in Pillay *et al*'s words, engaged in 'active construction of knowledge' but they wanted reassurance that they were progressing along the right lines.

We end this section with some comments from a group of apprentices in the chemical industry, who remind us that some contemporary workplaces still operate on Fordist lines with perhaps just a touch of Orwellian overtones:

> Ben: They do keep tabs on how everyone is doing you know, the higher up people as well, look to see if you're doing well or anything.

> Gary: And there's Mr Z who's the training co-ordinator.

> Pete: He's got a lovely little office, high in the sky, he can see everything that goes on in the workshop.

Assessors and assessment

As we noted earlier in this chapter, apprentices are expected to be assessed in the workplace for their NVQ level 3 and for key skills. Some of this assessment may be done by colleagues in the workplace and some may be carried out by college or training provider staff coming into the workplace. For both the NVQ and key skills, assessment involves being observed carrying out a specific activity and via written evidence of the performance of a range of tasks, collected in a portfolio.

In the first extract, three apprentices in the steel industry explain how they collect evidence for key skills:

> Ben: Basically we collect evidence. We are given our standards, and we know how many pieces of evidence we've got to get. We collect evidence, bring it in (to the off-the-job training centre). We have meetings once every month. Then we collect more evidence and if he (the training officer) thinks it's good and fulfils the standard, he'll sign it off and that's a piece of evidence towards it.

> Int: And how do you collect the evidence?

> Ben: Well it's off our own bat really, we have to look at the standards and think where can we get this from... right I'll have a talk with one of the blokes at work and go and write it up and get him to sign it, if he has to sign it to say that we've had this discussion.

> Andy: You also have to show him the standard don't you, and say 'do you think what I've wrote here conforms with that standard'.

> Int: Do the blokes at work understand what they have to do?

> Andy: They do once you've showed them the standards. So, for Communication, well you explain that it's... you did your talk 'appropriately to the audience', so he'll just agree with that.

The discussion then broadened out from key skills to wider issues about workplace assessment.

> Int: What do you think of the assessment you've had in the workplace?

> Andy: It has been quite poor really.

> Chris: We haven't really had any what you'd say was in the workplace to be honest, not for NVQ.

> Ben: We've really tried to get NVQ level 3 together, trying to push them on. At the end of the day we can't get a modern apprenticeship certificate without the NVQ level 3, that's what we want, that is why we initially started out in this scheme.

> Int: What do you think would help improve things?

> Ben: Everything should be set out from when you first start, from day one, you should know what you are doing, what you've got to achieve, what you've got to get and then at the end of the four years, right, I've got that, I've got, that's it I've done, but like us we are coming up to our last year and our NVQ level 3 isn't even sorted out so you just feel a bit let down by that.

Andy: We could go to another company and we've said that we have done a modern apprenticeship and they might turn round and say well why haven't you got your modern apprenticeship because you haven't completed your level 3. That might be a reflection on us for being sloppy and not being bothered to get our NVQ level 3. From our point of view it's the workplace that is not actually implementing outside assessors for us. We just need to get on with it, at the moment we are at a bit of a standstill.

Int: Could a reason be that some of your firms have lost staff at different levels?

Chris: Yes, definitely that is what it is.

Int: Is the workplace actually up to doing this kind of assessment?

Andy: Oh yes definitely. At the moment you are doing jobs non-stop all the time, so there is opportunity there to get your evidence.

Ben: You could easily meet the standards, yes.

Chris: We are doing loads of jobs but it's having the people trained up to assess us.

Int: Do you think the people in the workplace, the supervisors and so on, are they up to being assessors? Are they capable of it?

Ben: I think they'd be capable.

Chris: It's whether they'd take it on or not.

Ben: Whether they'd actually take it on... I don't know whether they are bothered about that.

Int: Should they be offered a little incentive?

Andy: I think you'd have to get them to do it. Otherwise it might be seen as just another thing.

Ben: Another job that they've got to do.

Andy: Another responsibility.

Ben: Especially at the minute because blokes that have gone have left loads of jobs to be done by who is left.

Andy: The work force has been reduced that much that everyone is a lot busier.

As well as shortage of time for assessment on the job, the apprentices felt that there was still a major lack of awareness about and understanding of NVQs in the workplace:

> Ben: They are bringing all these new qualifications in that are work-based. I think people at work just think 'what are these?' Managers are probably clued up but none of the work force are willing to take it on and they don't know what NVQs are.

> Andy: I think some of the workplace have actually done NVQs on site.

> Chris: Yes but it's mostly staff isn't it that have done it at ours?

> Andy: Yes but like in our training workshop where we used to go, they used to have like evening courses offering NVQ to people.

> Chris: The problem is people think they're going to do a qualification like a City and Guilds but then they see it's an NVQ and it looks weird and it puts them off a lot.

The issues of lack of time for assessment, lack of assessors and lack of awareness about the NVQ system raised by the steel apprentices were echoed by all the apprentices we spoke to for our research. Even in the retail sector, which was one of the first to sign up to the new qualifications, the apprentices experienced problems in getting workplace assessors to keep up to date with the assessment. Two retail apprentices explained:

> Jane: You feel like you have to hassle them to get them to watch you do something and sign it off.

> Pete: I'd hate to have some trainee keep bothering me. Everyone is too busy, what with all the ordering and customers, and keeping the place tidy.

> Jane: They could just write a report on us, couldn't they, like once a month instead of having to assess us for every little thing.

It is noticeable here how the apprentices are conscious of the pressure that competence-based assessment is putting on their workplace colleagues whom they know have little, if any, time to spare during a busy day. The NVQ model makes trainees or 'candidates' responsible for seeking out an assessor as and when they feel ready to demonstrate their competence. Even if experienced workers had the necessary time to devote to NVQ assessment, it is still a tall order to expect young people to instigate assessment procedures. As our research shows, young people are anxious about their relationships with older colleagues in the workplace, and, in addition, they are attempting to socialize themselves into the culture and working norms of a complex environment. This is in line with Brown's (1997, p 61) view that:

> An individual learns through interaction and communication with others. The
> process of learning though does not generate a single type of interaction.
> Rather learning takes place in contexts in which there may be multiple dimen-
> sions to the nature of the interactions: there may be a host of working and
> other relationships that have an influence upon the learning process.

In many sectors, it was clear that the bulk of the assessment was carried out
in off-the-job settings and that it was off-the-job training personnel, as
opposed to staff in the workplace, who understood the competence-based
approach. Given that NVQs were first introduced in the late 1980s, it is
clear from the views of the apprentices we spoke to that, in some industries,
they are far from being the employer-led, work-based qualifications that
their designers envisaged. Field (1995, p 30) has argued that even to suggest NVQs are 'employer-led' is a fallacy and that they arose 'less because of
demand from those involved in managing labour than from the ideas and
aspirations of a small coalition of modernising civil servants and
highly-placed training professionals'. Williams and Raggatt (1998) have
built on Field's earlier analysis to argue that NVQs were seen as the answer
by policymakers in the 1980s to a range of problems, one of which was the
need to provide qualifications for the rising numbers of young unemployed
on the youth training scheme (YTS). It was thought that these young people,
many of whom had left school with few qualifications, would not be interested in college-based qualifications assessed in the traditional manner
through written examinations and coursework. Work-based assessment
was, therefore, seized upon as the way forward.

Conclusion

The data we present above show quite vividly that systematic, well-planned
mentoring, and structured, ongoing, assessment are not occurring as they
should on the modern apprenticeship. Mentoring is dependent upon personal, sometimes chance or fortuitous relationships, and meetings – as
opposed to carefully planned and monitored mentor–mentee contact time.
Assessment is equally *ad hoc*, depending on the willingness of an employee
to interact with an apprentice, or on the energy and enthusiasm of a young
person to 'bother' or 'hassle' a fellow worker. These pressures of the workplace, especially in the context of rapid staff change and 'down-sizing', miti-
gate against the planned, clearly defined and systematic programme of
mentoring, supervision and assessment that so many of the young people
we interviewed would value.

In Chapter 4, we drew on Lave and Wenger's socio-cultural model of a
community of practice. This has much to offer but it arises out of research
carried out in non-industrialized and often rural settings, for example
among Yucatec Mayan midwives in Mexico, and Vai and Gola tailors in

Liberia. Fuller and Unwin (1998), Guile and Young (1999) and Young (2000) argue that the model can be enhanced and made more relevant by embracing the ideas of Engestrom (1994; 1996), who draws insights from the Russian 'activity theorists' such as Vygotsky (1978) and Leontiev (1978). As Fuller and Unwin (1998) explain, 'activity theory':

> ...recognizes the extent to which people learn in social situations and through interaction, whilst at the same time suggesting that their knowledge and understanding can be further advanced through structured teaching and learning.

Engestrom (1994, p 48) argues that modern workplaces demand more than a reliance on people informally absorbing knowledge and skills for the achievement of *expansive* as opposed to *imitative* learning:

> ...although there are many occasions of productive learning in everyday situations, most of everyday learning consists of conditioning, imitation and trial and error. Investigative deep level learning is relatively rare without instruction or intentional self-instruction. For that very reason, instruction is necessary. Its task is to enhance the quality of learning, to make it purposeful and methodical.

Given that the quality of mentoring, supervision and workplace assessment is unpredictable on the modern apprenticeship, it is reasonable to speculate that young people in jobs that lie outside government-supported training programmes are even less likely to experience adequate care and attention. For many young people, starting work coincides with that time in their lives when they are trying to come to terms with who they are and what they want to be. For example, Mac an Ghaill (1999) has shown that young people have to struggle to understand and come to terms with the challenges that the workplace environment places on their emerging sexual identity. In a study of young men on the modern apprenticeship, he argues that they are often placed within a 'hyper-heterosexual arena', where they feel the need to demonstrate not just occupational competence, but sexual competence as well (see Lane, 1996, for a discussion of sex and apprenticeship throughout history). Young women, and men, may be confronted by sexual harassment from older and often more senior colleagues, and black and Asian young people may face racist attitudes.

Young people need to feel secure that appropriate mechanisms are in place, both on and off-the-job, to ensure they have access to properly trained assessors, mentors and supervisors. That the United Kingdom's flagship government-supported training programme is failing in this regard should be a matter of serious concern.

7

Building on young people's perspectives

Introduction

In this book we have tried to show how young people's perspectives on education, training and employment shed important light on the gap between policy rhetoric and lived experience. We have also shown that young people across the ability range are attracted to the work-based route in order to combine continued study with employment, and that they enjoy a mix of learning experiences.

As we travelled the country talking to young people, we were constantly surprised by their willingness to put up with a system that was hardly over-reaching itself to serve them. The serendipitous route by which many young people had joined the modern apprenticeship was illustrative of the haphazard way post-16 provision is matched to individual need and desire. There must be countless young people labouring on the wrong course in full-time education or attempting to progress in the wrong occupational sector or stuck with an employer who fails to see their potential. There are many, too, of course, who are not even in the system and whose potential lies dormant. We also saw plenty of successful partnerships and some excellent examples of good practice. There is, however, more than enough room for improvement and young people have a great deal to tell us about how the system could and should be developed.

In this concluding chapter, we will try to bring together a number of themes that have emerged in the book and suggest the policy lessons that might be drawn.

Young people's post-school vision

The first point to make in any analysis of this kind is that one is very conscious of making dangerous generalizations. Clearly young people and their circumstances differ greatly. The young people in our research were relatively successful. They had all achieved enough examination passes at 16 to gain access to a modern apprenticeship. Some of them had gained access to apprenticeships with prestigious employers and were set on a route that would lead to university and certainly management level jobs within their companies. Their typicality lies in the fact that they had all attended state schools and had faced, at 16, the decision as to which pathway to take. Like most of their peers, they were subject to pressures and advice from parents, teachers, relatives, and friends. They had listened to careers officers. Several of them, again like many of their peers, had tried more than one pathway in the search for the one that would suit them best.

Evans (1998, p 60) explains this behaviour in terms of 'navigation', a metaphor that emerged during the 1990s to describe how people were having to become more reflexive in order to cope with an increasingly post-modern world; thus, Evans talks of how 'individuals are navigating perilous waters and negotiating their way in a sea of "manufactured uncertainty"' (Evans, 1998, p 60). Here Evans borrows the term 'manufactured uncertainty' from Giddens (1991). The young people we spoke to were crossing and re-crossing a number of boundaries in their navigations both during and after compulsory schooling: between school and part-time work; full-time work and college; work and social life. Yet, it has perhaps been overlooked that, although it is certain that such busy navigation is occurring, these young people are still hoping to find firm land on which to rest for part of the time. They are aware of the fragility of the labour market and do not expect, as older generations did, a 'job for life' but, we would argue, they should be entitled to some stability during their formative years as young adults.

If we are to support young people in their decision making and ensure that policymaking responds to their needs, then we have to listen to young people as they articulate the world as they see it. We have to listen to them interpret much of the rhetoric that is perpetrated on their behalf and use that interpretation to challenge our own assumptions about why and how young people choose certain routes and not others. There is a perception among policymakers that young people's decision making operates within a paradigm of choice supported by careers guidance. The reality, however, is that decision making is a highly pressurized process during which both young people and their parents struggle to make sense of the pathways on offer and their various divisions. The astonishing variability in the quality of government-supported training programmes and full-time academic and vocational educational provision is something about which the websites, leaflets and glossy brochures have nothing to say.

The young people to whom we spoke seemed to have a realistic grasp of the advantages and disadvantages of the various post-16 routes on offer to them although, for some, that realism had been acquired the hard way by trying out different pathways and finding them wanting. The realism also stems from the collected wisdom available through their own networks –

friends and relations report back on how they have experienced certain routes – and partly from a pragmatic approach to life in general. A 16 year old will look at the options open to him or her and ask several straightforward questions:

- What *status* will I have among my peers, community and family if I take pathway X?
- What will pathway X lead me to?
- Will pathway X provide me with any financial support and, if not, can I survive if I choose that pathway?
- Can I cope with pathway X or is it really aimed at a different sort of person from me?
- Will my parents approve?
- Will pathway X lead me into debt?
- Will pathway X get me, perhaps eventually, into a 'proper' job?
- Does the qualification offered at the end of pathway X have any credibility with employers or universities?

The following summarizes how young people judge the pathways.

Status of post-16 pathways

- *Full-time education* (A-levels, resit/improve GCSE results, GNVQ, other vocational qualifications, mix of academic and vocational such as GNVQ plus A-level). Offers/represents: status in community – better to be a student than an apprentice in a poorly regarded occupational sector with a bad employer; better than being unemployed. Chance of a future, possibly an interesting course *but* also relative financial instability (unless lucrative part-time work can be found). There is no guarantee of success in result terms – for example, a student may end up with two useless A-levels. A GNVQ won't necessarily get a student into the higher education institution of his or her choice. There are some dodgy curriculum concoctions.
- *Part-time education*. As above. Linked to employment training. Offers/represents: depends on the type of employment package it is linked with or, if there is a personal arrangement, it may mean that there is a chance for the student to reassess what he or she wants to do long-term.
- *Legal employment* (full-time or part-time job plus training). Offers/represents: status in community, money, chance of a future – if training included then status rises.
- *Employment in the informal labour market* (a temporary job with erratic hours). Offers/represents: instant financial reward (sometimes relatively high) and freedom, *but* may have health and safety risks and will not offer any substantive training.
- *Modern apprenticeship* (employed status plus training to a minimum level of NVQ 3). Offers/represents: possible status depending on type of

employer it is linked to – for example, a big name employer means that the apprenticeship will be recognized in the community. It could lead to long-term advancement. It probably pays a reasonable wage.

- *National traineeship* (employed or trainee status plus training to a minimum level of NVQ 2). Offers/represents: little status and often derision from community; low pay if on state allowance as opposed to wage; less than 50 per cent chance of achieving a qualification; possibly a permanent job. However, could get an NT with a company that sees it as a route to the apprenticeship and so NT could be worthwhile.

The apprentices we spoke to said they wanted to combine the following within one pathway:

job + pay + training/studying + qualifications

This combination reflected the fact that these young people looked to the workplace as a fresh site for learning, somewhere that would be different from school and somewhere that could unlock their potential. As one group of apprentices memorably explained, the workplace would give them 'a chance to shine'. The workplace is now as familiar an environment to many teenagers as school or college, and we know that many so-called full-time students are working as many hours part-time as they are studying in a classroom. One interesting area for research would be to explore the ways in which young people learn in these different environments and whether they transfer any of that learning across the classroom/workplace boundaries.

The problem that young people in our research were finding, however, is that although every modern apprenticeship programme actually offers the very combination they desired, the quality of experience differs enormously.

Learning at work

We saw in Chapter 1, that the government has announced the following improvements to the modern apprenticeship:

- a clear apprenticeship structure, in which national traineeships become foundation modern apprenticeships (FMAs), leading up to advanced modern apprenticeships (AMAs);
- major improvements to the knowledge and understanding required from apprenticeship programmes, achieved by pulling together the range of technical qualifications to give clear accreditation to the underpinning skills and knowledge needed for the workplace;
- inclusion of a specified period of off-the-job learning in college, or with other training providers, with a suggested minimum of one day a week or equivalent;

- the specification of minimum periods of learning – for example two years for level 3 modern advanced apprenticeships, with entry requirements tightened up (DfEE, 2000e).

We would suggest that young people would welcome these improvements but that they would also highlight the failure on the part of government to address the following glaring inadequacies that bedevil the current programme:

- lack of adequate on-the-job support in the form of mentoring and supervision;
- lack of integration of on and off-the-job training;
- lack of adequate amounts of time available to devote to apprentices in pressurized workplaces;
- poor understanding of apprenticeship model in some workplaces;
- inadequate systems for ensuring proper assessment for NVQs and key skills.

The serious problems inherent in the model of key skills currently being deployed in full-time education as well as on the work-based route were documented in Chapter 5. We do not wish to rehearse those problems here but to simply state that there is a considerable gap between theory and the practice in relation to key skills. There is an important debate to be had about how, when and where these skills should be developed, the relationship between basic skills and key or generic skills, the validity of the concept that such skills naturally occur in all workplaces, and the relationship between these skills and workplace competence. At the moment, however, young people's impoverished experience of key skills will only serve to diminish a potentially valuable concept.

It is noticeable that the government's list has nothing to say about employer responsibility and commitment, but concentrates, instead, on the content and length of the programmes. Nor has the government anything to say about whether *all* employers should be allowed to deliver modern apprenticeships, or, for that matter, any form of government-supported training programme, or whether only certain employers should be licensed to train young people. On the contrary, the government takes a much more simplistic view, as the following extract from a leaflet to promote modern apprenticeship reveals:

> Young people must have access to the training that they deserve. Employers need more and more highly skilled employees. That's why we have set ambitious targets to ensure that all young people complete their training and that employers fully benefit from their investment.
>
> (DfEE, 2000e)

115

This suggests that the cards are all in the employers' hands. As we have seen from the experience of young people in this book, however, serious attention needs to be given to the question as to whether employer involvement in government-supported training programmes should be restricted. In terms of workplace environments, the apprenticeship experience will be very varied:

- their employer may have a long tradition of training, including apprenticeship, be very new to the demands of long-term training, or take the view that the training provider should shoulder the main responsibility;
- they may be working alongside a casualized workforce where older workers have little time or motivation to pass on their expertise;
- they may be the only trainees/apprentices on site;
- they may find little integration between their learning activities in the workplace and their off-the-job training programme;
- many of the sectors delivering the modern apprenticeship have no tradition of apprenticeship and their training experience might be largely confined to short-term, task-specific activities;
- their workplace personnel may not be capable of providing adequate learning and mentoring support.

The long-standing problem of inadequately trained trainers in the UK has been well documented and continues to hold back progress in workplace learning (see Brown *et al*, 1994; TSC, 1999). It is concerning therefore that the UK government has decided to give employers 'unprecedented influence over the (post-16) education system' (DfEE, 1999a, p.20) through the new learning and skills councils at national and local level.

The wide sectoral and employer spread of the apprenticeship means that apprentices can find themselves positioned along a considerably stretched continuum of experience:

Continuum of apprenticeship experience

Quality experience – minimum provision.
Sector with tradition/infrastructure – sector new to training.
Employer committed to training – employer ambivalence.
Member of community of practice – isolated.
Basket of qualifications – NVQ level 3.
Mentor /trained supervisor – lack of support.

There is, in essence, no guarantee at the moment that such a widely dispersed work-based pathway will deliver anything in terms of a quality holistic experience, but will simply attempt to fulfil the minimum framework requirement of, in the case of modern apprenticeship, attainment of an NVQ level 3, or in the case of national traineeship, an NVQ level 2, plus some key skills.

Current rhetoric surrounding national economic competitiveness and globalized patterns of industry and commerce tells us that employers are in need of more people with higher levels of skills. Ashton and Felstead's (1999, p 69) survey of skill trends in Britain presents a more realistic picture. They found that 'on average, better qualifications are required to get jobs and carry them out' and that 'jobs take longer to train for and take longer to learn to do well'. They argue, however, that despite evidence of upskilling for young and mature workers alike, there is a 'deficiency of employer demand' and so 'underused... human capital resources'. This suggests that the government needs to make a greater effort to develop work-based pathways that place young people with employers whose own needs are properly in line with the demands and expectations of those pathways, and who can provide a workplace environment that is conducive to apprenticeship-style training. Such a move would challenge the long-standing voluntarist approach to the employer/state relationship. Hodgson and Spours (1999, p 141) point out, however, that, since their election in 1997, the Labour government has shown little sign of accepting such a challenge and has maintained the 'weak framework approach to the labour market and training' of their predecessors, rather than emulating the social partnership (and hence 'strong') framework approach favoured by many other European countries.

This does not bode well for the government's latest proposal to develop foundation degrees as part of its drive to get 50 per cent of young people into higher education by the time they are 30. Launching these proposals, the Education Minister, Baroness Blackstone, said, 'The foundation degree will play a key role in this expansion of opportunity, creating a new vocational route into higher education' and explained that:

> The foundation degree will be a new qualification for a new century. It will strengthen the links between higher education and the world of work. It is a radical and direct response to employer demand for more and better trained technicians and associate professionals. The degree will deliver the specialist knowledge and skills which employers need, underpinned by rigorous and broad-based academic learning. The new two-year foundation degree will combine academic learning with practical skills and workplace experience. It will be available full-time or part-time, and we expect substantial numbers to choose the part-time route, combining study with a job. It is a significant step towards a robust ladder of vocational progression – a key strand of the Government's initial response to the recommendations of the National Skills Task Force.

> (DfEE, 2000f)

Again the emphasis here is on the content of the programme coupled with an assumption that appropriate and adequate learning environments already exist. We would argue, based on our research with young people, that if a quality work-based route existed, many would take it in preference to remaining in school or college. Developing the work-based route demands, however, a considerable shift away from New Labour's commitment to a voluntarist approach to employers. Hodgson and Spours (1999) and Evans *et al* (1997) argue that the government should embrace the social partnership policies of some other European countries in which employers, trades unions and government work together to produce robust vocational education and training structures.

Young people do, however, expect governments to at least try and deliver what they want. As one engineering apprentice said to us: 'Basically, what we want is to be able to go to work and study for a qualification that other employers will recognize and be able to work our way up so that we can do things like go to university if we want to. It's hardly rocket science.'

The dangers in being ordinary

The young people whose thoughts are portrayed in this book are in danger of being overlooked by both academics and policymakers. They are not part of the 'status zero' group of socially excluded youngsters and they are not working in the highly casualized end of the labour market. With luck, the majority of them should stay employed and some may even progress both occupationally and educationally. Yet they are suffering the consequences of a system that has still not given really serious attention to their needs or aspirations.

A further problem that this group faces is that the quality of the work-based pathways is largely evaluated using quantitative measures. The government collects statistics on the numbers of young people joining and leaving the pathways but does little to investigate the quality of their experience. The Training Standards Council (TSC) inspection reports provide valuable information but it is restricted to examining the quality of education and training providers servicing the work-based route. Very little has been done to investigate young people's experiences on employers' premises.

Opportunities to speak

We have tried to show in this book that listening to young people's perspectives is important as they expose the often-messy reality behind much education and training rhetoric. Furthermore, we would argue that bringing young people together in groups can be a highly effective means of encouraging them to reflect on their experiences. There is a sense in which this group reflection also makes the young people much more visible and, potentially, powerful. The problem is that opportunities for this to happen tend only to occur through the vehicle of a research project. There are no formalized 'youth committees' or 'youth forums' in operation, a situation not helped by the lack of any substantive involvement on the part of trade unions in the design and delivery of the work-based pathways.

In choosing to take the work-based pathway, a young person enters a paradoxical situation in which they are still part of the government-supported post-16 system but, unlike their peers in full-time education, they are largely left to get on on their own. Their situation is much more individualized than that of full-time students who retain a collective identity whether in school or college. Once young people enter the fragmented world of work, they are often isolated from their peers. There are opportunities for them to come together via off-the-job training sessions, and some, as we see in this book, may be in workplaces where there are small groups of apprentices and trainees, but their sense of being a 'group' is far less prominent than it would be for students in educational settings.

We are conscious of the danger of advocating formalized youth forums for which young people might not feel any ownership. We suggest, however, that ways must be found to allow young people to tell their stories and debate their experiences in order to make an active contribution to the design and delivery of the programmes and pathways they inhabit.

Appendix

Modern apprenticeship sectors	Enrolments to May 2000
Accountancy	9,708
Agriculture and garden machinery	392
Agriculture and commercial horticulture	2,095
Air transport	634
Amenity horticulture	1,038
Animal care	1,251
Arts and entertainment	94
Banking services	539
Broadcasting	79
Builders' merchants	234
Building services engineers	148
Bus and coach	545
Business administration	45,131
Ceramics	4
Chemicals industry	997
Cleaning and support services	51
Clothing	90
Construction	22,763
Craft baking	362
Customer service	17,476
Distribution and warehousing	584
Early years care and education	11,117
Electricity supply industry	495
Electronic system servicing	294
Electrotechnical industry	13,819
Emergency fire service	107
Engineering construction	1,162
Engineering manufacture	34,815
Environmental conservation	43
Farriery	7
Fibreboard	3
Floristry	263
Food and drink	94
Furniture manufacture	666
Gas industry	305
Glass	332

Guidance	7
Hairdressing	21,594
Health and beauty therapy	89
Health and social care	20,315
Heating, ventilation, air conditioning	2,131
Hospitality	25,579
Housing	83
Information and library services	7
Information technology	7,480
Insurance	807
International trade	434
Jewellery, silversmith and allied trades	1
Knitting, lace and narrow fabrics	15
Management	2,217
Man-made fibres	20
Marine industry	885
Meat industry	523
Merchant navy	14
Motor industry	23,955
Museums, gallery and heritage	20
Newspapers	251
Operating department practice	118
Paper and board manufacture	81
Personnel	62
Photography and photographic processing industry	61
Physiological measurement technicians	109
Plumbing	4,507
Polymers	149
Printing	2,982
Procurement	7
Rail	47
Residential estate agency	1,305
Retailing	28,253
Road haulage and distribution	302
Sea fish	23
Security	674
Signmaking	25
Sports and recreation	3,373
Steel industry	463
Surface coatings	4
Telecommunications	2,187
Textiles	312
Timber trade (wood machining)	86
Travel services	7,751
Water Industry	1

References

Ainley, P and Bailey, B (1997) *The Business of Learning*, Cassell, London

Ainley, P and Corbett, J (1994) From vocationalism to enterprise: social and life skills become personal and transferable', *British Journal of Sociology of Education*, **15** (3), pp 365–74

Ashton, DN (1986) *Unemployment under capitalism,* Wheatsheaf Books, Brighton

Ashton, DN and Green, F (1996) *Education, Training and the Global Economy*, Edward Elgar Publishing, Cheltenham

Ashton, DN, Maguire, MJ and Spilsbury, M (1989) *The Changing Structure of the Youth Labour Market*, Macmillan, London

Ashton, DN, Maguire, MJ and Spilsbury, M (1990) *Restructuring the Labour Market: The Implications for Youth*, Macmillan, London

Ball, S, Macrae, S and Maguire, M (1999) Young lives at risk in the futures market: some policy concerns from ongoing research, in *Speaking truth to Power*, ed F Coffield, The Policy Press, Bristol

Banks, M, Bates, I, Breakwell, G, Bynner, J, Emler, N, Jamieson, L, and Roberts, K (1992) *Careers and Identities*, Open University Press, Milton Keynes

Barrow, R (1987) Skill talk, *Journal of Philosophy of Education*, **21** (2), pp 187–99

Bates, I (1991) Closely observed training: an exploration of links between social structures, training and identity, *International Studies in Sociology of Education*, **1** (1), pp 224–43

Bates, I (1993) A job which is 'right for me'? Social class, gender and individualization, in *Youth and Inequality,* eds I Bates and G Riseborough, Open University Press, Buckingham, pp 14-31

Bates, I and Dutson, J (1995) A Bermuda Triangle? A case study of the disappearance of competence-based vocational training policy in the context of practice, *British Journal of Education and Work*, **8** (2), pp 41–59

Bates, I and Riseborough, G (1993) Deepening Divisions, Fading Solutions, *Youth and Inequality,* eds I Bates and G Riseborough, Open University Press, Buckingham, pp 1–13

Blake, D, Hanley, V, Jennings, M and Lloyd, M (1998) Mentoring in Action on a Primary PGCE Course, *Journal of Further and Higher Education,* **22** (3), pp 353–64

Bloomer, M (1997) *Curriculum Making in Post-16 Education: The social conditions of studentship*, Routledge, London

Bloomer, M and Hodkinson, P (1997) *Moving into FE: the voice of the learner*, Further Education Development Agency, London

Bradshaw, D (1985) Transferable intellectual and personal skills, *Oxford Review of Education,* **11** (2), pp 201–16

Bridges, D (1993) Transferable skills: a philosophical perspective, *Studies in Higher Education*, **18** (1), pp 43–51

Brooker, R and Butler, J (1997) The learning context within the workplace as percieved by apprentices and their workplace supervisors, *Journal of Vocational Education and Training*, **49** (4), pp 487–510

Brown, A (1997) A dynamic model of occupational identity formation, in *Promoting Vocational Education: European Perspectives*, ed. Heikkinen A, University of Tampere, Tampere, Finland

Brown, A, Evans, K, Blackman, S and Germon, S (1994) *Key Workers: Technical and training mastery in the workplace*, Hyde, Bournemouth

Burgess, T (1986) *Education for Capability*, NFER-Nelson, Windsor

Bynner, J (1998) Education for what? *Education and Training*, **40** (1), pp 4–5

Bynner, J, Ferri, E, Shepherd, P, Parsons, S, Joshi, H, Pierella, P, Smith, K, Montgomery, S, Schoon, I and Wiggins, R (eds) (1997) *Twenty-something in the 1990s: getting on, getting by, getting nowhere*, Ashgate, Aldershot

Campbell, M, Chapman, R and Hutchinson, J (1999) Spatial skill variations: their extent and implications, *Skills Task Force Research Paper 14*, DfEE Publications, Nottingham

CBI (1989) *Towards a Skills Revolution – a youth charter*, Confederation of British Industry, London

CBI (1996) CBI proposes skills passport to provide lifetime learning for all, *CBI News*, January, Confederation of British Industry, London, p 16

Clarke, L (1999) The changing structure and significance of apprenticeship with special reference to construction, in *Apprenticeship, Towards a New Paradigm of Learning*, (1999) (eds) P, Ainlay and H, Rainbird, Kogan Page, London

Cohen, P (1984) Against the new vocationalism, in Bates, *et al* (eds) *Schooling for the Dole? The New Vocationalism*, Macmillan, Basingstoke

Coleman, JC and Warren-Adamson, C (eds) (1992) *Youth Policy in the 1990s*, Routledge, London

Coles, B (1995) *Youth and Social Policy*, UCL Press, London

Dearden, L, McIntosh, S, Myck, M and Vignoles, A (2000) *The Returns to Academic, Vocational and Basic Skills in Britain,* Centre for Economic Performance, London School of Economics, London

Dearing, R (1996) *Review of 16–19 Qualifications*, Summary of the Interim Report, SCAA, London

Dench, S, Perryman, S and Giles, L (1998) *Employers' Perceptions of Key Skills*, IES Report 349, Institute of Employment Studies, Sussex

DES/DOE (1991) *Education and Training for the 21st Century*, Cmnd 1536, HMSO, London

DfEE (1999a) *Learning to Succeed,* Cm 4392, The Stationery Office, London

DfEE (1999b) *Modern Apprenticeship Database*, Department for Education and Employment, Sheffield

DfEE (2000a) *Participation in Education, Training and Employment by 16–18 year olds in England, 1998–99*, Statistical First Release, Department for Employment and Education, London

DfEE (2000b) *TEC/CCTE Delivered Government-Supported Training: Work-based training for young people and work-based learning for adults*, Statistical First Release, Department for Employment and Education, London

DfEE (2000c) *Secretary of State, Dvaid Blunkett's Speech to the Further Education Funding Council's Annual Conference*, February 16th 2000, Birmingham

DfEE (2000) *Work-Based Training for Young People and Work-Based Learning for Adults: Volumes and Outcomes*, Statistical First Release 26/2000, Department for Education and Employment, London

DfEE (2000d) *Connexions,* Department for Education and Employment, Nottingham

DfEE (2000e) *Vocational Education and Training: A framework for the future*, Department for Education and Employment, Sheffield

DfEE (2000f) *Call to employers, universities and colleges to take Foundation Degrees a step further*, Press Release, 10 July

Dunne, E and Bennett, N (1997) Mentoring processes in school-based training, *British Educational Research Journal*, **23** (2), pp 225–38

Edwards, T, Fitz-Gibbon, CT, Hardman, F, Haywood, R and Meagher, N (1997) *Separate But Equal? A Levels and GNVQs*, Routledge, London

Engestrom, Y (1994) *Training for Change*, International Labour Office, Geneva

Engestrom, Y (1996) Development as breaking away and opening up: a challenge to Vygotsky and Piaget, *Swiss Journal of Psychology*, **55**, pp 126–32

Eraut, M (1994) *Developing Professional Knowledge and Competence*, The Falmer Press, London

Evans, K (1998) *Shaping Futures, Learning for Competence and Citzenship*, Ashgate, Aldershot

Evans, K, Hodkinson, P, Keep, E, Maguire, M, Raffe, D, Rainbird, H, Senker, P and Unwin, L (1997) Working to Learn, *Issues in People Management*, No 18, Institute for Personnel and Development, London

Felstead, A and Green, F (1996) Training implications of regulation compliance and business cycles, in *Acquiring Skills,* eds A Booth and D Snower, Cambridge University Press, Cambridge

Felstead, A and Unwin, L (1999) *Funding Systems and their Impact on Skills*, Skills Task Force Research Paper II, Department for Education and Employment, Sudbury

Fergusson, R and Unwin, L (1996) Making Better Sense of Post-16 Destinations: a case study of an English shire county, *Research Papers in Education*, **11** (1), pp 53-81

Field, J (1995) Reality testing in the workplace: are NVQs 'employment-led'?, in *The Challenge of Competence*, (eds) P Hodkinson and M Issitt, Cassell, London

Finegold, D and Soskice, D (1988) The failure of training in Britain: analysis and prescription, *Oxford Review of Economic Policy*, **4** (3), pp 21–51

Fuller, A (1996) Modern Apprenticeship, Process and Learning: some emerging issues, *Journal of Vocational Education and Training*, **48** (3), pp 229–48

Fuller, A and Unwin, L (1998) Reconceptualising Apprenticeship: exploring the links between work and learning, *Journal of Vocational Education and Training*, **50** (2)

Fuller, A and Unwin, L (1999) A sense of belonging: the relationship between apprenticeship and community, in *Apprenticeship, Towards a New Paradigm of Learning* (1999) (eds) P, Ainley and H, Rainbird, Kogan Page, London

Furlong, A (1992) *Growing Up in a Classless Society? School to Work Transitions*, Edinburgh University Press, Edinburgh

Furlong, A and Biggart, A (1999) Framing 'choices': a longitudinal study of occupational aspirations among 13–16 year olds, *Journal of Education and Work*, **12** (1), pp 21–35

Giddens, T (1991) *Modernity and Self-Identity: Self and society in the late modern age*, Polity Press, Cambridge

Gleeson, D and Hodkinson, P (1995) Ideology and curriculum policy, GNVQ and mass post-compulsory education in England and Wales, *British Journal of Education and Work*, **8** (3), pp 5–19

References

Gleeson, D, Glover, G, Gough, G, Johnson, M and Pye, D (1996) Reflections on youth training: towards a new model of training experience? *British Educational Research Journal*, **22** (5), pp 597–613

Gray, J, Jesson, D and Tranmer, M (1993) *Boosting Post-16 Participation in Full-time Education: A study of some key factors in England and Wales*, Youth Cohort Study No. 20, Employment Department, Sheffield

Green, A (1997) Core skills, general education and unification in post-16 education, in *Dearing and Beyond*, (eds) A, Hodgson and K Spours, Kogan Page, London

Griffin, C (1993) *Representations of Youth: The Study of Youth and Adolescence in Britain and America*, Polity Press, Cambridge

Guile, D and Young, M (1999) Beyond the institution of apprenticeship: towards a social theory of learning as the production of knowledge, in *Apprenticeship, Towards a New Paradigm of Learning*, eds P Ainley and H Rainbird, Kogan Page, London

Harris, S (1997) Partnership, community and the market in careers education and guidance: conflicting discourses, *International Studies in Sociology of Education*, **7** (1), pp 101–19

HMSO (1995) *Competitiveness Forging Ahead*, Cm 2867, HMSO, London

Hodgson, A and Spours, K (eds) (1997) *Dearing and Beyond, 14–19 Qualifications, Frameworks and Systems*, Kogan Page, London

Hodgson, A and Spours, K (1999) *New Labour's Educational Agenda*, Kogan Page, London

Hodkinson, P (1996) Careership: the individual, choices and markets in the transition into work, in *Knowledge and Nationhood*, eds J Avis, M Bloomer, G Esland, D Gleeson and P Hodkinson, Cassell, London

Hodkinson, P and Issitt, M (1995) (eds) *The Challenge of Competence,* Cassell Education, London

Hodkinson, P, Sparkes, A and Hodkinson, H (1996) *Triumphs and Tears: Young People, Markets and the Transition from School to Work*, David Fulton, London

Holt, M (ed) (1987) *Skills and Vocationalism: the easy answer*, Open University Press, Milton Keynes

Huddleston, P (1999) Modern apprentices in college: so what's new? In *Apprenticeship, Towards a New Paradigm of Learning*, eds P Ainley and H Rainbird, Kogan Page, London

Huddleston, P and Unwin, L (1997) Skills, stakeholders and star-gazing: the relationship between education, training and the economy, in *Qualifications for the Future*, eds G Stanton and W Richardson, FEDA Strategic Research, Vol 2, No 5, Further Education Development Agency, London

Hyland, T (1994) *Competence, Education and NVQs: Dissenting perspectives*, Cassell, London

Instance, D, Rees, G and Williamson, H (1994) *Young People Not in Education, Training or Employment in South Glamorgan*, South Glamorgan Training and Enterprise Council, Cardiff

Jessup, G (1991) *Outcomes, NVQs and Emerging Models of Education and Training*, The Falmer Press, London

Jessup, G (1993) Towards a Coherent Post-16 Qualifications framework: the role of GNVQs, in *The Reform of Post-16 Education and Training in England and Wales,* eds W Richardson, J Woolhouse and D Finegold, Longman, Harlow

Jonathan, R (1987) The Youth Training Scheme and Core Skills: An educational analysis, in *Skills and Vocationalism: The easy answer*, (ed) M, Holt, Open University Press, Milton Keynes

Jones, G and Wallace, C (1992) *Youth, Family and Citizenship,* Open University Press, Buckingham

Keep, E (1992) Designing the stable door: a study of how the Youth Training Scheme was planned, *Warwick Papers in Industrial Relations*, No 8, University of Warwick, Coventry

Keep, E (1999) UK's VET policy and the 'third way': following a high skills trajectory or running up a dead end street? *Journal of Education and Work,* **12** (3), pp 323–46

Keep, E and Mayhew, K (1999) The assessment: knowledge, skills and competitiveness, *Oxford Review of Economic Policy,* **15** (1), pp 1–15

Kolb, D (1984) *Experiential Learning: Experience as the source of learning and development*, Prentice-Hall, Englewood Cliffs, NJ

Kvale, S (1996) *Interviews: An Introduction to Qualitative Research Interviewing*, Sage, Thousand Oaks CA

Labour Party (1996) *Aiming Higher: Labour's proposals for the reform of the 14–19 curriculum*, Labour Party, London

Lakoff, G and Johnson, M (1980) *Metaphors We Live By*, University of Chicago, Chicago

Lane, J (1996) *Apprenticeship in England 1600–1914*, London, UCL Press

Lave, J (1993) The practice of Learning, in *Understanding Practice*, (eds) S, Chaiklen and J, Lave, Cambridge University Press, Cambridge

Lave, J and Wenger, E (1991) *Situated Learning*, Cambridge University Press, Cambridge

Lee, D, Marsden, D, Rickman, P and Duncombe, J (1990) *Scheming for Youth, A Study of YTS in the Enterprise Culture*, Open University Press, Buckingham

Leontiev, AN (1978) *Activity, Consciousness, and Personality*, Prentice-Hall, Englewood Cliffs, NJ

Levine, PB and Zimmerman, DJ (1995) A comparison of the sex-type of occupational aspirations and subsequent achievement, *Work and Occupations*, **22** (3), pp 73–84

Lucas, R and Lammont, N (1998) Combining work and study: an empirical study of full-time students in school, college and university, *Journal of Education and Work,* **11** (1), pp 41–56

Lyotard, J F (1984) *The Postmodern Condition: a Report on Knowledge* (trans G Bennington and B Massumi), Manchester University Press, Manchester

Mac an Ghaill, M (1999) 'New' cultures of training: emerging male heterosexual identities, *British Educational Research Journal,* **25** (4), pp 427–43

Macdonald, B and Rudduck, J (1971) Curriculum research and development projects: barriers to success, *British Journal of Educational Psychology*, **41**, pp148–54

McCulloch, G (1989) *The Secondary Technical School: A Usable Past?*, Falmer Press, Lewes

MSC (1984) *Core Skills in YTS, Part 1: Youth Training Scheme Manual*, Manpower Services Commission, Sheffield

NCC (1990) *The Whole Curriculum*, Curriculum Guidance 3, National Curriculum Council, York

NSTF (1999) *Towards a National Skills Agenda*, Skills Task Force First Report, Department for Education and Employment, Sudbury

NSTF (2000) *Skills for All: Proposals for a National Skills Agenda*, Skills Task Force Final Report, Department for Education and Employment

Payne, J (1998) *Routes at Sixteen: Trends and Choices in the Nineties*, Department for Education and Employment, Sheffield

References

Pearce, N and Hillman, J (1998) *Wasted Youth*, Institute for Public Policy Research, London

PEPI (1993) *Personal Effectiveness Programme Initiative*, Janet Jones Associates Ltd, London

Pring, R (1995) *Closing the Gap: Liberal Education and Vocational Preparation*, Hodder & Stoughton, London

QPID (2000) *Mentoring for Work Based Training*, QPID Study Report No81, DfEE, Sheffield

Raffe, D (1986) *The context of the Youth Training Scheme: An analysis of its strategy and development*, Centre for Educational Sociology, Working Paper No. 8611, University of Edinburgh, Edinburgh

Raggatt, P and Williams, S (2000) *Government, Markets and Vocational Qualifications*, Falmer Press, London

Rees, T (1992) *Women and the Labour Market*, Routledge, London

Richardson, W (1993) The 16–19 education and training debate: 'deciding factors' in the British public policy process, in *The Reform of Post-16 Education and Training in England and Wales*, eds W Richardson, J Woolhouse and D Finegold, Longman, Harlow

Roberts, K (1995) *Youth Employment in Modern Britain*, Oxford University Press, Oxford

Rudduck, J, Harris, S and Wallace, G (1994) Coherence and students' experience of learning in the secondary school, *Cambridge Journal of Education*, **24** 2, pp 197–211

Ryan, P (1999) The embedding of apprenticeship in industrial relations: British engineering, 1925–65, in *Apprenticeship, Towards a New Paradigm of Learning*, eds P Ainley and H Rainbird, Kogan Page, London

Ryle, G (1949) *The Concept of Mind*, Hutchinson, London

Senker, P (1992) *Industrial Training in a Cold Climate: An assessment of Britain's training policies*, Avebury, Aldershot

SEU (1999) *Bridging the Gap: New Opportunities for 16-18 year olds not in education, employment or training*, Report by the Social Exclusion Unit, Cm 4405, The Stationery Office, London

Sherlock, D (1999) Modern apprenticeship and national traineeship – raising standards, speech to *Training for Young People, Skills for the Millennium Conference*, Hinckley, Leicestershire, 13th and 14th September, Conference Report, TEC National Council

Smith, R (1998) *No Lessons Learnt: a Survey of Social Exclusion*, The Children's Society, London

Spours, K (1995) *Post-compulsory Education and Training: Statistical trends*, Learning for the Future Working Paper No. 7, Post-16 Education Centre, Institute of Education, University of London, London

Spours, K (1997) GNVQs and the future of broad vocational qualifications, in *Dearing and Beyond, 14–19 Qualifications, Frameworks and Systems*, eds A Hodgson and K Spours, Kogan Page, London

Stern, E and Sommerlad, E (1999) *Workplace Learning, Culture and Performance*, Institute of Personnel and Development, London

Stronach, I (1989) Education, vocationalism and economic recovery: the case against witchcraft, *British Journal of Education and Work*, **2** (1), pp 5–31

Stronach, I and Maclure, M (1997) *Educational Research Undone, The Postmodern Embrace*, Open University Press, Buckingham

Stronach, I and Morris, B (1994) Polemical notes on educational evaluation in the age of 'policy hysteria', *Evaluation and Research in Education*, **8** (1/2), pp 5–19

Stronach, I and Torrance, H (1995) The future of evaluation: a retrospective, *Cambridge Journal of Education*, **25** (3), pp 283–99

TSC (1999) *Chief Inspector's Report*, Training Standards Council, London

Unwin, L (1991) NVQs and man-made fibres industry: a case study, in *Change and Intervention: Vocational Education and Training*, eds P Raggatt and L Unwin, The Falmer Press, London

Unwin, L (1993) Training credits: the pilot doomed to succeed, in *The Reform of Post-16 Education and Training in England and Wales*, eds W Richardson and D Finegold, Longman, Harlow

Unwin, L (1996) Employer-led realities, *Apprenticeship Past and Present*, 48 (1), pp 57–68

Unwin, L (1997) Reforming the work-based route: problems and potential for change, in *Dearing and Beyond*, eds A Hodgson and K Spours, Kogan Page, London

Unwin, L (1999) *Jungle Trekking: Vocational Courses and Qualifications for Young People*, Skills Task Force Research Paper 5, Sudbury: Department for Education and Employment

Unwin, L and Wellington, J (1995) Reconstructing the Work-Based Route: Lessons from the Modern Apprenticeship, *Journal of Vocational Education and Training*, **47** (6), pp 337–52

Unwin, L and Wellington, J (1997) 'Personal Effectiveness' as a cross-curricular goal: catalysts, barriers and varying perceptions, *Pastoral Care*, **15** (2) pp 1–5

Venables, E (1974) *Apprentices Out of Their Time*, Faber & Faber, London

Vygotsky, LS (1978) *Mind in society: the development of higher psychological processes*, Harvard University Press, Cambridge

Watts, M and Ebbutt, D (1987) More than the sum of the parts: research methods in group interviewing, *British Educational Research Journal*, **13**, pp 25–34

Wellington, J (1992) Varying perspectives on work experience, *The Vocational Aspect of Education*, **44** (2), pp 153–82

Wellington, J (1993) (ed) *The Work-Related Curriculum*, Kogan Page, London

Wellington, J (1994) How far should the post-16 curriculum be determined by the needs of employers? *Curriculum Journal*, **5** (3), pp 309–21

Whitty, G, Rowe, G and Aggleton, P (1994) Discourse in cross-curricular contexts: limits to empowerment, *International Studies in Sociology of Education,* 4 (1), pp 25–42

Widdecombe, A (1993) Government's view for the future, speech to the CBI Youth Credits Conference, *Learning from Experience*, 1 December

Williams, S and Raggatt, P (1998) Contextualising public policy in vocational education and training: the origins of competency-based qualifications in the UK, *Journal of Education and Work*, **11** (3), pp 275–92

Wolf, A (1991) Assessing core skills: wisdom or wild goose chase? *Cambridge Journal of Education*, **21** (2), pp 189–202

Wolf, A (1995) *Competence and Assessment*, Open University Press, Buckingham

Wolf, A and Silver, R (1990) *Measuring 'broad' skills: the prediction of skills transfer and retention over time*, Mimeo, University of London Institute of Education, London

Young, MFD (2000) Bringing knowledge back in: towards a curriculum for lifelong learning, in *Policies and Practices in Lifelong Learning*, ed A Hodgson, Kogan Page, London

Index

Index

www.ingramcontent.com/pod-product-compliance
Ingram Content Group UK Ltd.
Pitfield, Milton Keynes, MK11 3LW, UK
UKHW010020280225
455677UK00023B/721